Zuni Fetish Carvers of the 1970s

A BRIDGE FROM PAST TO PRESENT

Kent and Laurie McManis

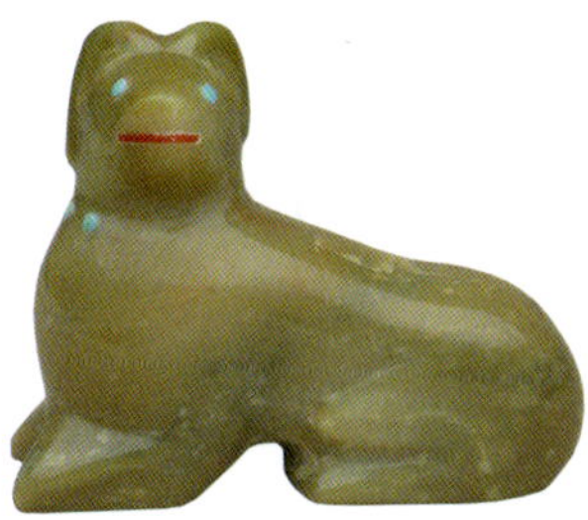

Published by the
Wheelwright Museum of the American Indian
704 Camino Lejo, Santa Fe, NM 87505
www.wheelwright.org

Published in conjunction with an exhibition of the same title, June 25–October 30, 2005

Edited by Cheri Falkenstien-Doyle and Jonathan Batkin

Designed by David Skolkin

Printed by Colorado Printing

All photographs by Robin Stancliff except page 58, figure 3 by Addison Doty.

CONTENTS

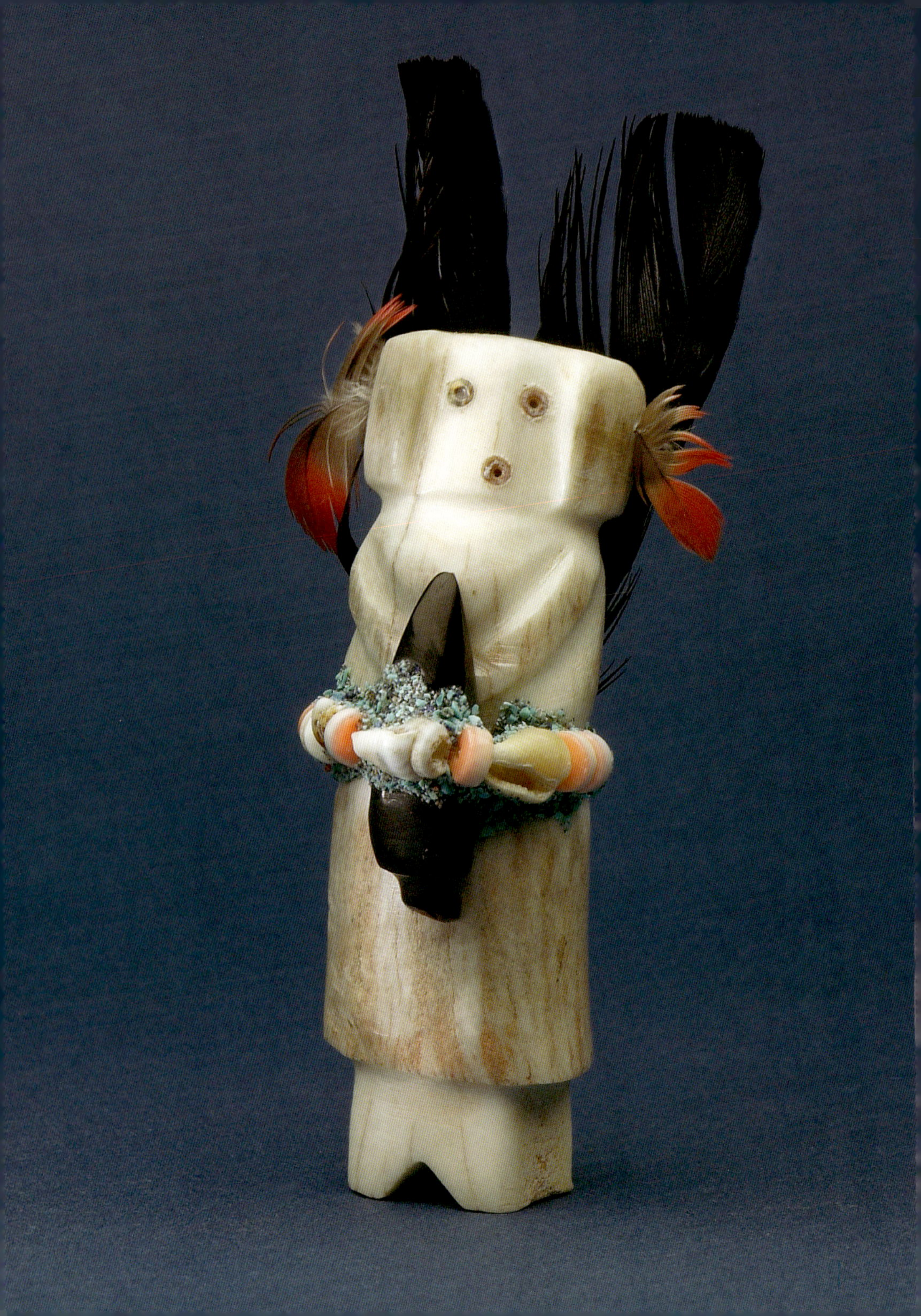

FOREWORD

IN 2003 THE WHEELWRIGHT was honored to publish Kent McManis' *Zuni Fetish Carvers: the Mid-Century Masters*. That book, based in part upon the Wheelwright's Leonora Scott Curtin collection, told the story of the first generation of Zuni carvers to make fetishes as a secular art form. We were pleased when Kent proposed to us the project represented here—an exhibition and book documenting the next generation of carvers, who nurtured the craft and paved the way for the tremendous popularity it enjoys today.

This book, like its predecessor, is important for its attention to the artists' points of view. Kent's research consists of many hours of interviews with carvers and their families, and with the traders and dealers who have sold their work. These books come out of oral histories, and could not exist without the enthusiastic participation of Zuni's carving community. Their insights regarding the artistic and economic climate of the pueblo during the 1970s, as well as their willingness to share biographical detail and family photos, have been essential. We are grateful to them, and to the many collectors who loaned more than 200 fetishes, necklaces, and other objects to the exhibition.

Finally, we thank Kent and Laurie McManis for a thoughtful manuscript that reflects their passion for Zuni carving, and their affection and respect for the people of Zuni Pueblo. Our appreciation for their patience, generosity of spirit, and unfailing good humor cannot be overstated.

CHERI FALKENSTIEN-DOYLE
Curator

ACKNOWLEDGMENTS

AN EXHIBITION AND BOOK LIKE THIS come about through the contributions, expertise, and good will of countless people. We want first to thank the hard-working corps of the Wheelwright Museum of the American Indian in Santa Fe. To Jonathan Batkin, Cheri Falkenstien-Doyle, Mary Katherine Ellis, Leatrice Armstrong, and Willow Powers go much appreciation for encouraging a second fetish exhibition to follow the successful *Zuni Fetish Carvers: The Mid-Century Masters* (2003), thereby honoring the next generation of carvers. *Elahkwa* to the gracious Zuni people who allowed us access to their memories of thirty years ago. Some of those wonderful people include Nita and Randolph Yuselew, Ernest Bewanika, Juanita Tucson, Eddie Hannaweeke, Saul Yuselew, Lucy Ohmsattie, Marvelita Phillips, Reva Halate, Bernard Homer, Jr., Juana Homer, Sarah Leekya, Ricky Laahty, Angelena Laahty, Charles and Rosalie Hustito, Vivian and Terry Johnson, Lena Boone, Peter and Dinah Gasper, Sandra Gregory, Anderson Weahkee, Bobby and Clifford Lonasee, Delia and Estefanita Ponchuella, Lawrence and LoRae Lonasee, Georgette Quam, Reynold Lunasee, Andres, Faye, Sandra, and Stewart Quandelacy, Albenita Yunie, Lynn and Jayne Quam, Thelma and Lorandina Sheche, Jessie LeBouef, Marnella Kucate, Bill Tsikewa, Leonard and Lavina Kaskalla, Lorencita Mahkee, Gibbs Othole, Arvella Latone,

Rena Othole, and from the A:shiwi A:wan Museum and Heritage Center, Valerie Epaloose and Curtis Quam.

To Fabian Vicenti, Sr., and the staff of the Pueblo of Zuni Tribal Census Office, gratitude for help on spellings, relationships, and longevities. Special thanks to Governor Arlen Quetawki of Zuni Pueblo for providing the access to information so vital to completing the exhibition. Special appreciation to traders Pat Harrington, Greg Hofmann, Chet Jones, Joe and Cindy Tanner, Elaine Dodson Thomas, and Joe Douthitt for their help and expertise on the period. To all those who loaned fetishes to the exhibition, a debt of gratitude. Obviously, we couldn't have done it without their generosity. Extra special thanks to Robin Stancliff for her continued ability to bring the experience of the exhibit to the pages of this book. Laurie wishes to express her eternal gratitude to M. B., to her sister, Dayl Brenneman, for teaching her about beauty, and to Ken Blackman, for his ceaseless inspiration and support. And finally, we wish to express our heartfelt thanks to all of these amazing Zuni fetish carvers for keeping the art alive and strong during a time of near extinction. We only wish all of them could have been here to enjoy this exhibit. Perhaps in fact they are, through their wonderful families and creations.

—Kent and Laurie McManis

INTRODUCTION

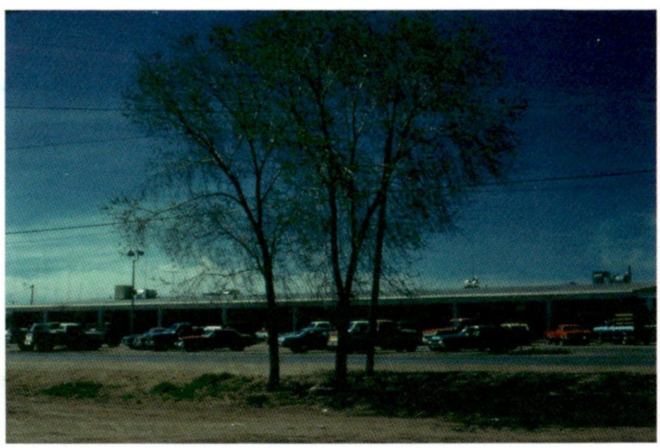

Zuni tribal building, circa 1979. Photograph by John Adair. Wheelwright Museum of the American Indian.

THE 1970S were a breakthrough period in Native American art. Stimulated in part by the civil rights movement of the 1960s, which focused national attention on social, economic, and political issues important to native peoples, the popularity of pottery, textiles, jewelry, and other traditional art forms grew tremendously. Jewelry in particular became highly fashionable—a phenomenon many traders, including Chet Jones of Zuni's Pueblo Trading Post attribute to the hippie movement, with its romantic idealization of American Indian spirituality and fascination with exotic fashion.

In 1974 *Arizona Highways*, a publication of the Arizona Department of Transportation, released several issues that focused on Native American art. Among the diverse and talented artists featured in the series were jewelers such

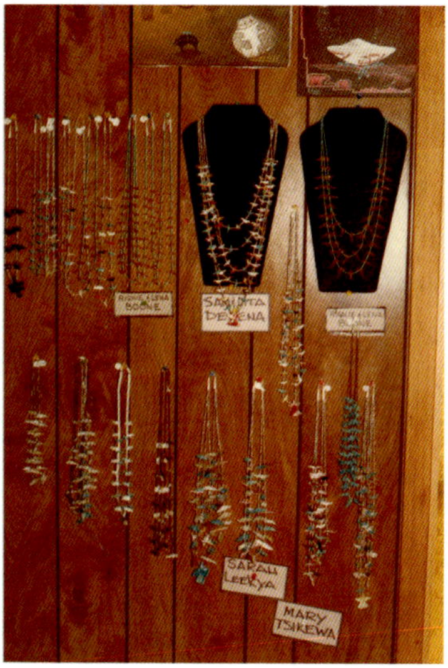

Stringing fetishes for sale at Turquoise Village, circa 1979. Collection of Greg Hofmann, Turquoise Village.

as Charles Loloma and Preston Monongye—craftsmen whose work displayed a degree of sophistication and a contemporary edge that few people besides dealers in American Indian art had seen. These publications were highly influential and helped to expand the market for jewelry beyond that of every other American Indian art form.

Zuni fetishes grew in popularity as well, particularly in the form of fetish necklaces. A few artists had produced these commercially since the 1940s, but by the 1970s almost every carver who made free standing fetishes also made tiny birds and animals to be strung on necklaces—"stringing" fetishes. New carvers entered the field, demonstrating the continuing viability of the craft, but they were greatly outnumbered by jewelers.[1] Retailers who sold Native American art focused heavily on jewelry, devoting little space to fetishes. Even shops at Zuni offered few fetishes for sale.

The village of Zuni had few outlets for art in the 1970s, but among the most important was the Zuni Craftsmen Cooperative Association, known as the Co-op. Founded in 1967 with the help of a grant from the U. S. Office of Economic Opportunity, the Co-op was established in part to oversee quality control in Zuni crafts. In the mid-1960s several traders sold poor grade turquoise to jewelers in the village, and lied about its quality. Jewelry made with this turquoise began to give Zuni work a bad reputation. The tribal government enacted an ordinance to end this degradation, and the Co-op was founded shortly thereafter with the purpose of selling genuine, high-grade materials to Zuni artists. Its board included Albert Pewya, Jr. (president), Fred Bowannie, Sr. (vice-president), Patrick Tsethlikai (secretary), Tom Weahkee, and Edward Laweka. Originally located in the old Head Start building, the Co-op also marketed Zuni arts and offered classes in silversmithing. One of the first instructors was Peter

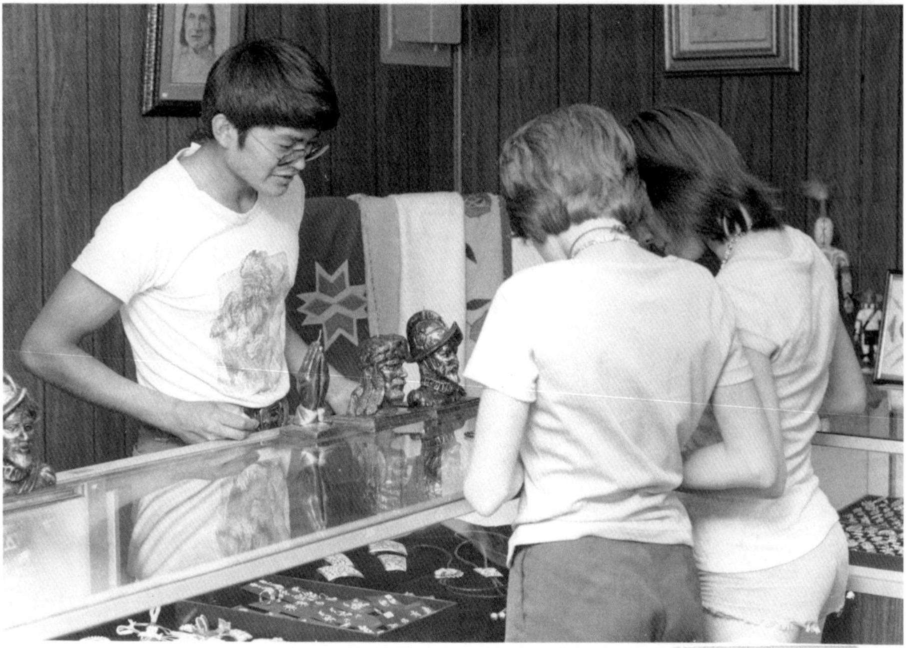

Gibbs Othole waiting on customers at the Zuni Craftsmen Cooperative Association, circa 1975. Collection of the A:shiwi A:wan Museum and Heritage Center.

Gasper, Sr., whose fetishes are included in this publication. Lena Boone, another carver whose work is featured here, worked as a salesperson and in the Co-op offices.

Arvella Latone, who has worked at the Co-op off-and-on since the mid-1970s, remembers that the shop carried a few fetishes by such artists as Old Man Acque, Edna Leki, Lena Boone, Alice Homer and her son, Bernard Homer, Jr., Leonard Halate, Leonard Kaskalla, and several members of the Quandelacy family. She recalls perhaps one shelf devoted to the display of fetishes.

Traders working at Zuni during that time have similar recollections. Pat Harrington began traveling to Zuni in 1969, buying art that he sold to retailers in Arizona and New Mexico as a means of making money for college tuition.[2] He remembers buying quantities of jewelry, but no more than one or two standing fetishes per trip. While stringing fetishes were somewhat more important to his inventory, he believes that standing fetishes represented 5 percent or less of his sales. He purchased fetishes from Saul Yuselew and his brother-in-law Harvey Bewanika, Aaron and Thelma Sheche, Rignie and Lena Boone, and the Quandelacy family. The carvings he bought in the 1970s differed from those made today in that they were less detailed, and he remembers that there were considerably fewer from which to choose.

Greg Hofmann opened his store, Turquoise Village, in 1978. He and his partner sold Sleeping Beauty turquoise from Arizona and other jewelers' supplies in about a quarter of the building he now fully occupies. Hofmann remembers selling fetish necklaces and a few standing fetishes, mostly by Peter and Dinah Gasper and Leonard Halate.

Lorencita Mahkee worked for Richard Vander Wagen at Hawikuh Trading, on the site of the current Mustang Store, from 1959 to 1977. She recalls that standing fetishes represented less than 5 percent of their business, and that stringing fetishes accounted for just a bit more. On the other hand, she remembers that the store stocked countless boxes of jewelry. Lorencita has worked for almost every arts and crafts dealer in Zuni, and says that standing fetishes never really caught on until the mid-1980s.

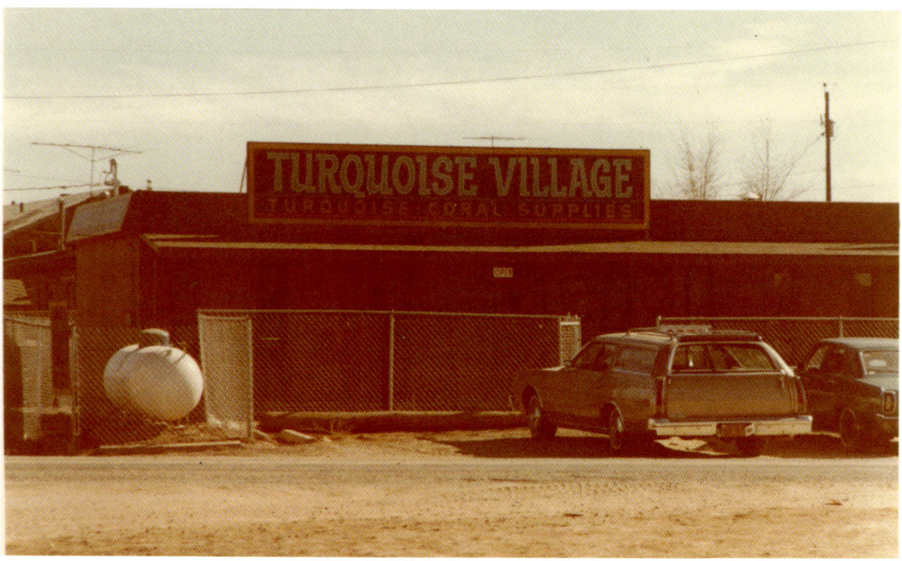

Turquoise Village, circa 1979. Collection of Greg Hofmann, Turquoise Village.

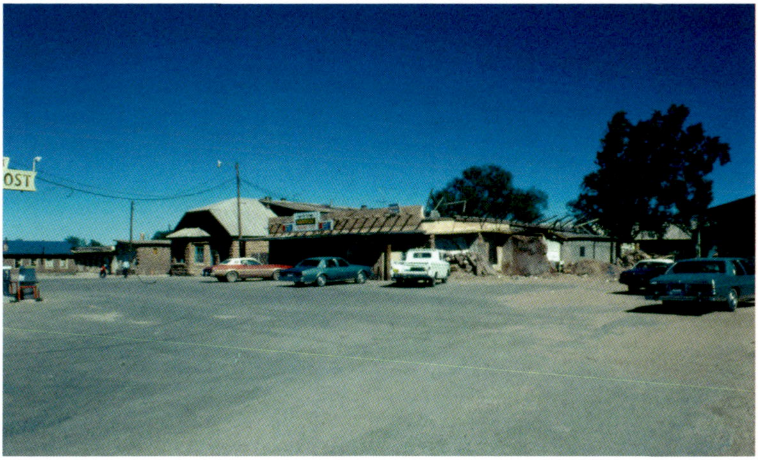

Hawikuh Trading Post, circa 1979. Photograph by John Adair. Wheelwright Museum of the American Indian.

Chet Jones began selling artists' materials and supplies door-to-door at Zuni in the early 1970s, before setting up shop in a trailer near the Co-op's current location. (He bought his current business, the Pueblo of Zuni Trading Post, after the "boom.") In those days, according to Chet, most traders were "roadrunners" and "day traders" who came to Zuni infrequently and stayed only a day at a time. They did little business in fetishes, and 90 percent of that was in carvings for necklaces. He suspects that as little as 1 percent of his own business was in standing fetishes.

Jones's partner at the time, Joe Douthitt wholesaled Zuni art, primarily to retailers in Tucson, but sometimes on the road. Joe remembers that stringing fetishes by Peter and Dinah Gasper sold for five to ten dollars apiece—a premium compared to the work of other carvers, which fetched no more than a dollar or two. He also recalls that standing fetishes made up a small percentage of his total sales.

With this exhibition and catalog, we hope to shift the focus away from jewelry, and to foster an appreciation of Zuni fetishes made during the 1970s. The artists whose work is featured here kept fetish carving alive when making jewelry was a far more lucrative occupation. Some of these carvers learned their craft long before the jewelry craze, and remained active well into old age. Many gave up careers as jewelers and devoted themselves to making fetishes instead.

Others took pride in carrying on the tradition of a noted father, husband, or other relative who pioneered the art during the first half of the twentieth century: they developed distinctive family styles that underscored the influence of the past upon the present. Some carvers discovered this artistic path on their own, creating a new tradition for their family or friends to follow.

Most of the fetishes featured in this catalog date to the 1970s, and all were made between about 1965 and 1985. Although the period of time under discussion is only thirty years in the past, it was difficult to locate and identify works by many artists. To attribute works accurately, we submitted each piece selected for the exhibition to the carvers' families and friends, and when possible to the carvers themselves, for verification.

In presenting this project, we pay tribute to those Zuni artists who kept an age-old tradition moving forward when it easily could have passed into history. They provided the continuity that has enabled fetish carving to thrive in subsequent decades, and by sustaining both the artistic and religious aspects of the craft, they bridged the gap from past to present, creating a solid and varied body of work upon which future carvers might build.

NOTES

1. By 1967, when the Zuni Craftsmen Cooperative Association was founded "to facilitate the manufacture and sale of Zuni silver jewelry, . . . 90 percent of the men and women were involved [in making jewelry] to some degree." Eggan and Pandey, 1979:479.

2. Harrington's parents, Bob and Helen, soon began to work with Patrick, and the three stayed in business together until Bob's passing in 1988 and Helen's in 1990. McManis, 2003:12.

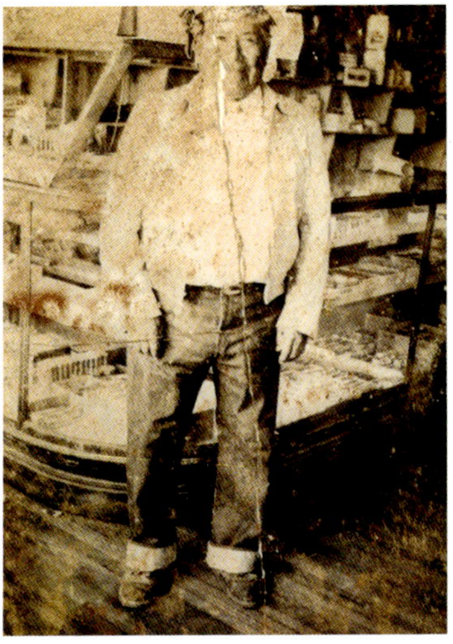

Old Man Acque at Kelsey's Store, date unknown. Kelsey's was an early trading post at Zuni. Collection of Nita Yuselew.

OLD MAN ACQUE

Old Man Acque (1888–1981), as he was known at Zuni, made simple, traditional carvings reminiscent of an earlier era. His fetishes seem friendly and approachable, and convey their subject matter with subtlety. By the 1970s Old Man Acque was undoubtedly the oldest carver still working, although nobody knows exactly when he began carving. His stepdaughter Nita Yuselew remembers watching him carve when she was quite young, so it is possible that he started in the 1940s. Like other carvers of his generation he used a hand-pumped drill, a hand-cranked grinding wheel, rasps, and files; and he used shears to chip off pieces of rocks. Working with hand tools was tedious and time-consuming, but according to his family he resisted using an electric buffing wheel, and instead polished fetishes painstakingly on his knee with a greased rag.

Although he usually carved bears, Old Man Acque sometimes made horses, which he traded to Navajos who used them as talismans to keep their own horses safe and healthy. On occasion he made wolves or coyotes as well. He especially liked working in serpentine, which he purchased from the Vander Wagens. In return he sold much of his work to them. He also used sandstone and other rocks found near Zuni. His style changed little over time, but as he grew older and carving became more challenging, his fetishes lost some of their roundness and took on a sharp-edged look.

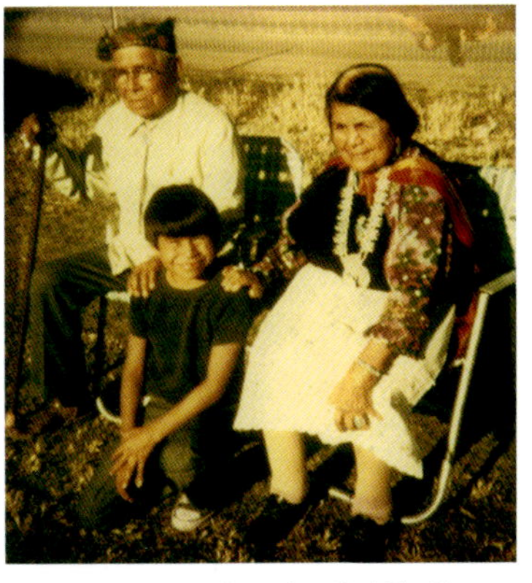

Old Man Acque with unidentified Zuni boy and woman, circa 1976. Collection of Nita Yuselew.

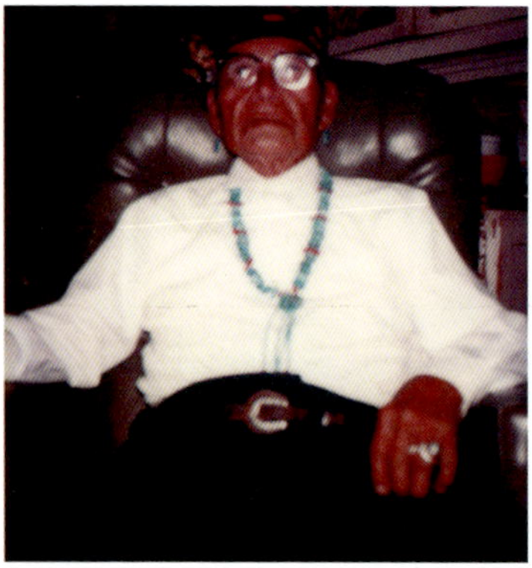

Old Man Acque, circa 1978. Collection of Nita Yuselew.

Old Man Acque was rare among fetish carvers in that, except for fetish necklaces, he never made jewelry. He was a farmer and a well-known storyteller, but he earned his living from fetish carving and sheepherding. Most importantly, his family proudly notes, Old Man Acque was also a religious leader.

He carved until he had a stroke in the late 1970s, not long before his death. Many of his descendants have honored his example by becoming carvers. These include Dinah Gasper, Fred Bowannie, Jr., Garrick Acque, and Randolf Yuselew.

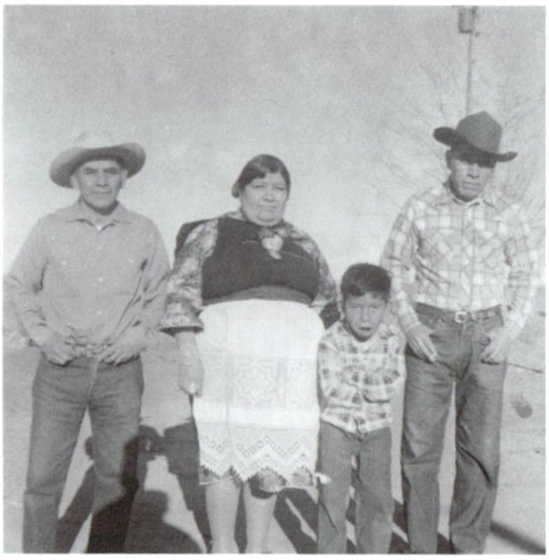

Saul Yuselew, Dena Yuselew, Edison Bobelu, and Harvey Bewanika, circa 1959. Collection of Saul Yuselew.

HARVEY BEWANIKA AND SAUL YUSELEW

Harvey Bewanika (1914–1987) remains one of the least-known fetish carvers of his generation. Harvey began making fetishes in the early 1970s. He and his brother-in-law Saul Yuselew shared a workroom, and for a time lived on opposite sides of the same house. Harvey carved his first fetishes from local rocks he found while tending his sheep. As time went on he began to produce fetishes for sale. At first Harvey used a hand-cranked grinding wheel, and later he acquired a modern electric polishing wheel, but carver Eddie Hannaweeke remembers that most of the time Harvey worked like the old-time carvers, with rasps and files. Harvey's son Ernest Bewanika remembers the high polish Harvey achieved on his pieces, and, for the 1970s, the correspondingly high prices he received for his work.

Harvey created a variety of animals, but seemed especially fond of bears. He enjoyed working with many types and hues of serpentine, but occasionally he used pipestone or antler. His fetishes are known for their distinctive dot motifs and inlaid mouths. He sold most of his work to the Harringtons and to Gallup trader Tobe Turpen.

According to his daughter Juanita Tucson, Harvey divided his time between carving fetishes and herding sheep. Many people at Zuni remember him running sheep through the village. He lost the sight in his right eye, but in spite of this he continued to carve. Eventually however his compromised vision took its toll, and in the early 1980s he quit carving.

Harvey was divorced, but Juanita remembers that he cherished all of his children, and did many kind things for them. Some of his descendants are silversmiths, but none carve fetishes today.

Saul Yuselew (1913–) is probably the oldest living fetish carver at Zuni, and many collectors covet his work for its unaffected charm. Although he began carving fetishes while in his teens, Saul worked as a jeweler throughout most of his adult life. But during the 1970s he switched to fetish carving full-time. As he grew older he found it difficult to execute the meticulous lapidary work characteristic of Zuni jewelry and preferred to work with larger pieces of stone. His early fetishes, many of which he sold to the Harrington family, had inlaid eyes, but by the 1990s Saul began to omit them, saying it had become difficult for him to form "good ones."

Bears have been Saul's favorite subject matter throughout his career, but he carves frogs, birds, and mountain lions as well. Today, perhaps at the urging of collectors, he carves a greater variety of animals than ever before. He has simplified his style over time, and his work is less highly polished than it once was. In many ways the fetishes he carves today suggest the essence of his earlier work: they are less detailed, but still convey each creature's form and personality.

Today Saul works with great- and great-great nieces and nephews, passing his skill along to a new generation of artists including Ricky Vacit, Jr., Avery Ohmsattie, and Sherrie Ohmsattie. It is interesting to note that his descendants often omit the eyes from their carvings too. Saul is a living treasure at Zuni, still working with an enthusiasm that defies the passing of time.

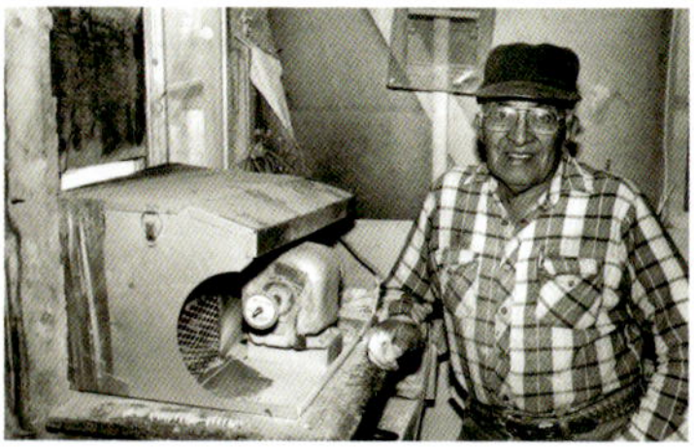

Leonard Halate at his work table, circa 1985. Collection of Reva Halate.

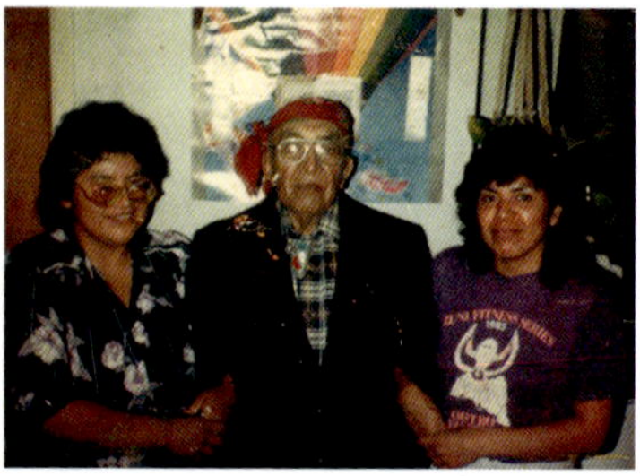

Marvelita Phillips, Leonard Halate, and Vella Halate, circa 1989. Collection of Marvelita Phillips.

LEONARD HALATE, PATRICK AND MARVELITA PHILLIPS

Leonard Halate (1914–2001) carved in a unique style that might best be described as folk art. His works are characterized by whimsy, humor, and a precarious sense of balance. Although he tackled traditional fetish animals with aplomb, he never seemed restricted by tradition, and became known for his interpretations of exotic creatures. Collected by many, Leonard's work was greatly appreciated in his later years.

Like many Zunis, Leonard was a farmer who raised sheep and cattle. He began carving fetishes in the 1960s. Until that time he worked as a jeweler, specializing in cluster bracelets for a Gallup trader named Carmelo Chiaramonte. When Chiaramonte asked if he could carve fetishes, Leonard began a new career. Fetish necklaces marked his entree into the field, and Turney's Indian Goods in Gallup, among others, marketed his work. Leonard carved for more than 30 years but stopped in the late 1990s because of heart problems that eventually took his life.

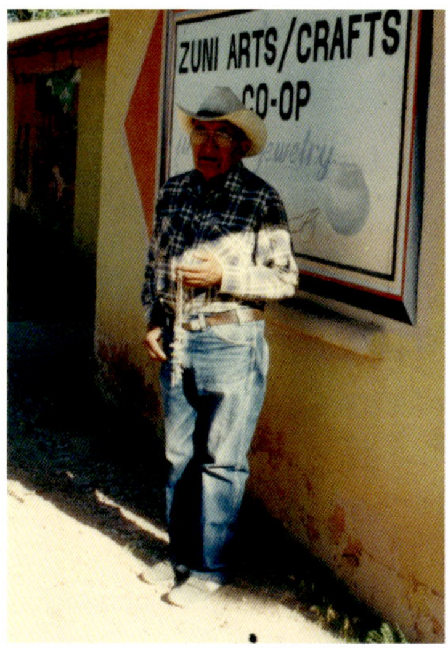

Leonard Halate at the old Co-op building holding one of his necklaces, circa 1988. Collection of Reva Halate.

Leonard especially enjoyed working in serpentine and antler. He fashioned a variety of animals including bears, wolves, mountain lions, rams, and even elephants. He is fondly remembered for the engaging dinosaurs and alligators he made of antler, however these were late additions to his repertoire. No one in his family remembers what motivated him to carve such unusual fetishes.

Leonard and his wife, Lena Martinez Halate, had four children: Reva Halate, Vella Halate, Herbert Halate, and Marvelita Phillips, all of whom began carving in the early 1970s. Leonard's adopted daughter and son-in-law, Pansy and Peter Natachu, Sr., also began at about this time. Marvelita's husband Patrick Phillips started carving before she did, apparently independently, after first specializing in inlaid jewelry. At that time Marvelita made cluster jewelry; but one night while Patrick was gone she carved a bear, a fox, and a bird. At first she hid her work, but when Patrick discovered it he encouraged her, and she also began to make fetish necklaces.

Early in their careers Marvelita (1951–) and Patrick (1940–) sold their work to Leon Ingraham of Zuni Sacred Mountain in Gallup, to Turney's, and to Stan Bartos and Frank Turpen of Gallup, who were both known for fostering Navajo imitations of Zuni fetishes. Patrick rarely carves today, but Marvelita still enjoys making bears, foxes, water serpents, and owls. Her signature pieces are groupings of owls and other birds made of antler, and "altar dolls," which while inspired by the carved figures of Teddy Weahkee, she says are more like Corn Maidens. Leonard Halate's other descendants, including several grandchildren, also carve. Their styles vary from "folk art" to polished, stylized work.

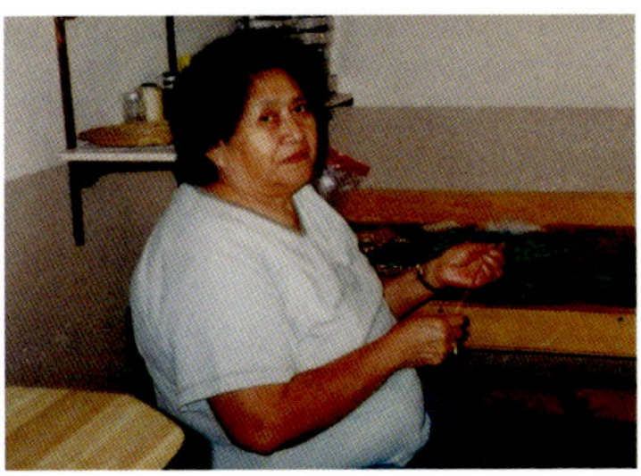

Sarah Leekya, circa 2000. Collection of Kent McManis.

ALICE HOMER, BERNARD HOMER, JR., SARAH LEEKYA, AND SADIE LAAHTY

Alice Homer (1923–1988) learned to make fetishes from her father, Leekya Deyuse, one of Zuni's best-known carvers. Alice began her career as a jeweler specializing in channel inlay, and probably made her first fetishes in the 1960s. According to her family, traders urged her to carve in order to perpetuate her father's legacy. Starting in the 1970s, and with increasing frequency in the 1980s, Alice created distinctive bears and wolves, which, while reminiscent of her father's, have a distinct style all their own, with idiosyncratic straight snouts. She preferred to work in Zuni rock (a local yellow or grey travertine), pipestone, serpentine, and alabaster. Her most frequent buyers were Turney's, Tobe Turpen, and trader John Kennedy in Gallup; and Greg Hofmann and the Vander Wagens in Zuni. After Alice's death from heart disease her children, Bernard Homer, Jr., Juana Homer, and the late Patrick Homer, all carried on the family's carving tradition.

Late in Leekya Deyuse's life, his grandson Bernard Homer, Jr. (1944–) helped him polish his fetishes. Inspired by his grandfather, Bernard took up carving in the 1960s, about the time that Leekya died. His first fetishes were bears, and soon he began to make birds. For his early work he used Zuni rock and serpentine, materials traditionally favored by his family. He still enjoys carving bears but has expanded his favorite materials to include turquoise, azurite-malachite, and lapis. Bernard's fetishes have a notched or "furrowed" brow that is their most diagnostic trait.

Leon Ingraham bought Bernard's first carvings, soon followed by Chet Jones, the Harrington family, and Joe Tanner, among others. Bernard's style has evolved since he began to carve. The Leekya family styles live on through his popular carvings and those of his sister Juana, who began making fetishes in the late 1980s, after a career as a jeweler. At this writing, Juana's daughter, Alicia Weahkee, is just beginning to carve.

Another daughter of Leekya Deyuse, Sarah Leekya (1930–) started carving in the mid-1960s, having helped her father sand and polish fetishes while she was still in school.[1] Sarah was a jeweler who made channel-inlaid rings and earrings, and well into the 1970s she continued to produce both jewelry and fetishes. When she found that she consistently had more orders for fetishes, she all but stopped making jewelry and devoted her time to carving. To this day she occasionally makes jewelry.

Sarah began her carving career by making stringing fetishes, primarily in bird forms. Later she also produced standing fetishes, but she continues to string necklaces today. While her style differs from that of her father, she conveys some of the same spirit in her work. Her early animal carvings often had slightly upturned snouts, and her birds' beaks were less elongated than those on Leekya's birds.

Sarah sold much of her early work to C. G. Wallace and Bernie Vander Wagen. Birds are still her favorite creatures to carve, and she prefers working in Zuni rock, as did her father, who used the stone so frequently that many Zunis refer to it as "Leekya rock." Unfortunately Zuni rock is not very accessible, and it is difficult for Sarah Leekya to retrieve it.

In addition to Alice Homer, Sarah's brothers and sisters include jewelers Elizabeth, Robert, and Roger, and the late Francis Leekya, who began carving seriously in the 1990s, at an advanced age and after a long career as a jeweler. Sarah is the family's last living carver of her generation.

Sadie Laahty (1926–1990) was the wife of carver and jeweler Morris Laahty. She and her husband spent most of their careers together producing channel-inlaid jewelry in their distinctive "sun face" design. Like Morris, Sadie carved fetishes infrequently, starting in the 1970s after Morris had already begun. She made a few standing animals, but more often carved birds to be strung on necklaces. She sold her work to Pat Harrington and Leon Ingraham. Sadie died in 1990, three years after Morris. Sadie and Morris left a legacy of fine jewelers in children Andrew, Arthur, Angelena, Andrea, Loretta, and Lorena. Their son Ricky Laahty is one of Zuni's great contemporary carvers.

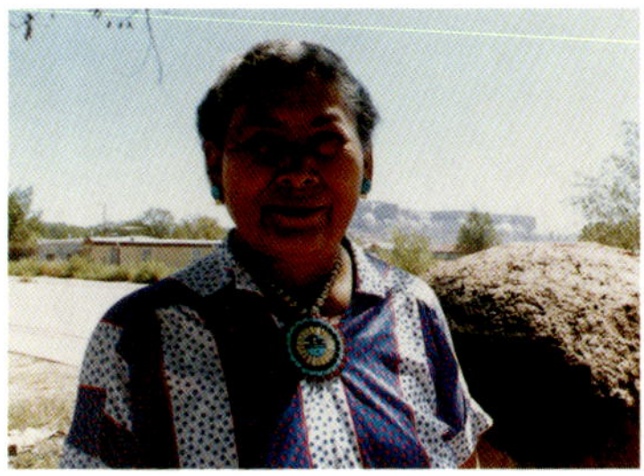

Sadie Laahty, date unknown. Collection of the Laahty Family.

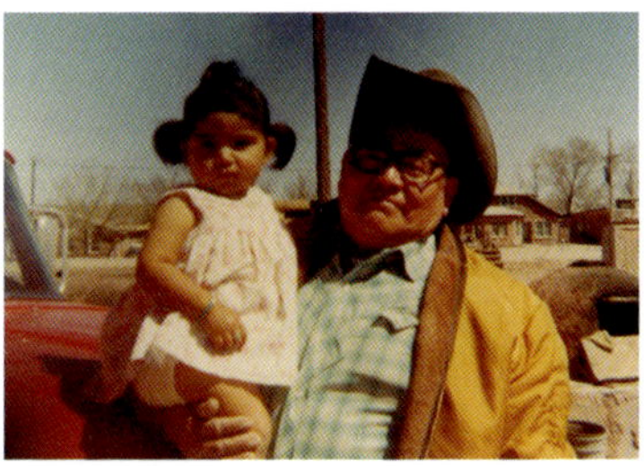

Alonzo Hustito holding his granddaughter, Kandess Hustito, circa 1967. Collection of Charles Hustito.

ALONZO AND CHARLES HUSTITO

Alonzo Hustito (1903–1987) began carving fetishes sporadically in the 1950s. A Zuni religious leader who also raised cattle and sheep, Alonzo is best remembered as a silversmith who created the settings for jewelry made by his wife Helen. Alonzo's first fetishes were made with hand tools, but he acquired electric tools in the 1970s. He was known for simple owls and bears, and for frogs and turtles that he often set into silver squash blossom necklaces and other jewelry. He carved almost until the time of his death, and passed his skills on to his children, who included jewelers Jason Hustito, Martha Shebola, Linda Wheeler, Vivian

Johnson, and Irma Eustace. Alonzo's son Charles Hustito is the only fetish carver of the group.

Charles Hustito (1941–) began carving in about 1972 at the age of 31, after serving in the army from 1965 to 1967, and as a tribal judge from 1969 to 1971. Like his father, he most often used serpentine and turquoise, which he carved in a simple, traditional style. He began making bears, which became a favorite subject matter, partly because of his father's influence. Charles produced most of his work during the 1970s. He has carved infrequently during the last few years, though occasionally he still makes bears and frogs. Today Charles tends sheep and spends most of his artistic time polishing the channel-inlaid jewelry of his wife, Rosalie Hustito. Charles's son Clive Hustito carves, as do his grandsons Jonas and Matthias. All add considerably more detail to their work than did either Charles or Alonzo.

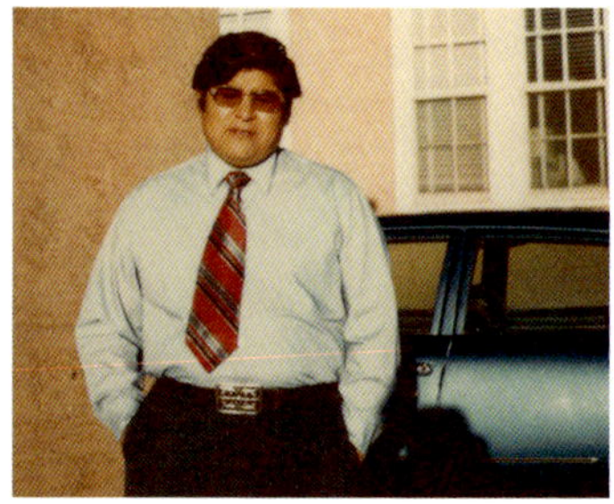

Zuni Tribal Judge Charles Hustito at Zuni tribal buildings, circa 1971. Collection of Charles Hustito.

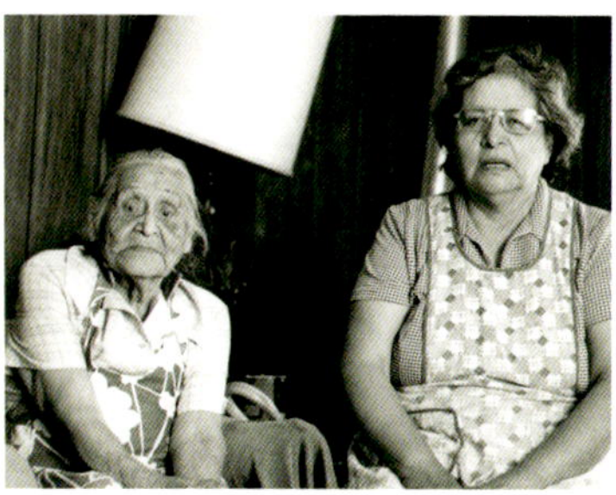

Anna Left Hand Weahkee and her daughter, Edna Leki, circa 1975. Collection of Lena Boone, Dinah Gasper, and Sandra Gregory.

EDNA LEKI, PETER AND DINAH GASPER, AND RIGNIE AND LENA BOONE

Edna Leki (1923–2003) was probably the first female fetish carver at Zuni, and certainly the first to pursue the craft full-time. She began carving in the late 1950s after attending the Santa Fe Indian School. Originally a maker of channel-inlaid jewelry, she gave this up in order to help her father, the famous carver Teddy Weahkee, make fetishes after he became ill. She assisted him until his death in 1965, after which she focused on her own career. Like most carvers of her generation, she made her first fetishes with a hand-cranked grinding wheel. Edna sold her early work to Joe Tanner, C. G. Wallace, and John Kennedy, as well as the Harringtons and the Vander Wagens. During her career

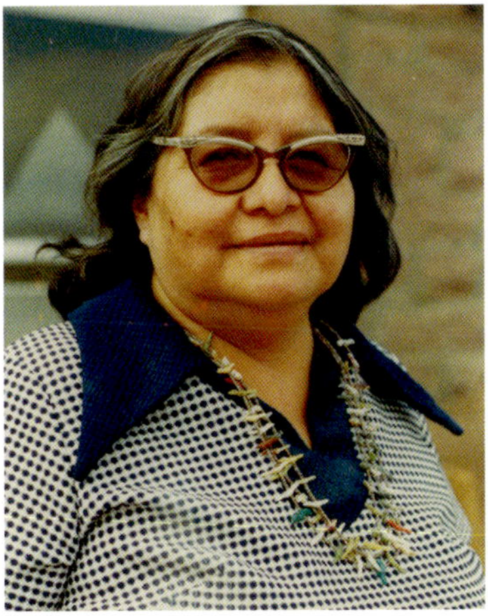

Edna Leki wearing one of her fetish necklaces, circa 1975. Collection of Lena Boone, Dinah Gasper, and Sandra Gregory.

she also strung squash blossom necklaces for C. G. Wallace at his trading post in Zuni.

Not all of Edna's animal carvings are representational, and some can be difficult to identify. Her mountain lions are particularly mystifying. She seems to have made more wolf fetishes than any other kind, but she made a variety of animals, most of them traditional. Although she used many kinds of stones, the various types of serpentine were clearly her favorites. She carved human figurines after her father's innovation, calling them "altar dolls." Edna's style resembled that of her noted father, especially during the early part of her career, and it changed only gradually over the years. Edna stopped carving around 1999 when her eyesight failed.

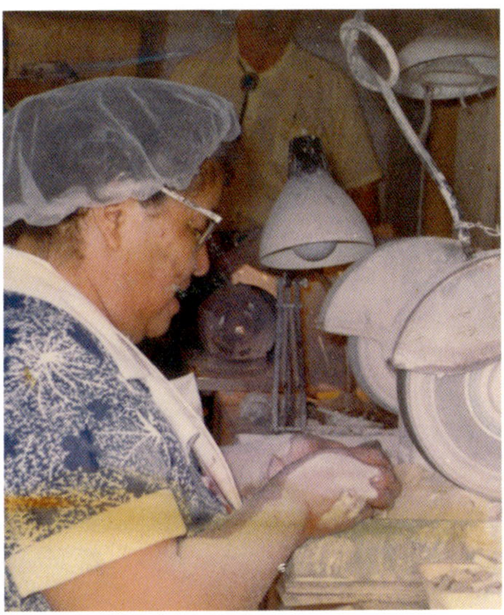

Edna Leki working on her fetishes, circa 1975. Collection of Lena Boone, Dinah Gasper, and Sandra Gregory.

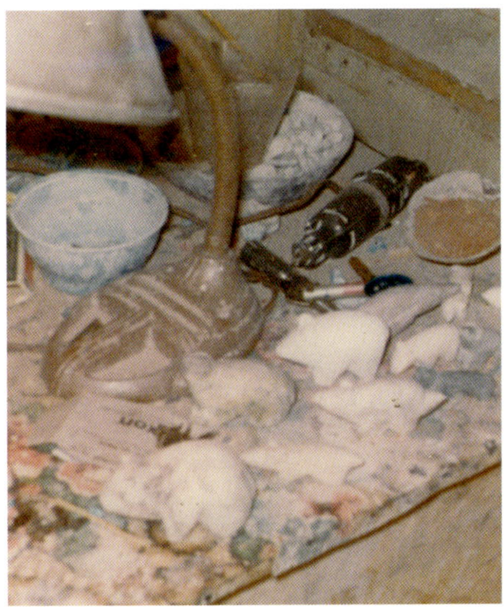

Edna Leki's fetishes in progress, circa 1975. Collection of Lena Boone, Dinah Gasper, and Sandra Gregory.

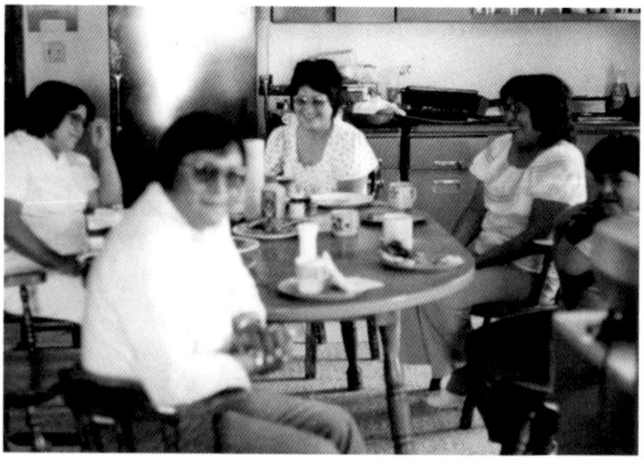

Dinah Gasper, Robert Michael Leki, Lena Boone, Sandra Gregory, and Leland Boone, circa 1975. Collection of Lena Boone, Dinah Gasper, and Sandra Gregory.

Peter (1938–) and Dinah Gasper (1944–) became carvers through the influence of Dinah's family. She is a granddaughter of both Old Man Acque and Teddy Weahkee, and the daughter of Edna Leki. Dinah worked with Teddy Weahkee during the late 1950s, drilling shells and helping to assemble the bundles that characteristically adorn his works. After Teddy's death she helped Edna make fetishes. Peter worked with Edna as well, helping to sand and polish her fetishes, and both Dinah and Peter sometimes helped Old Man Acque. Peter particularly remembers helping him make fetishes from antler. Before he began carving in 1968, Peter also worked for the USDA Forest Service and as an instructor of silversmithing for the Zuni Craftsmen Cooperative Association.

At the urging of a trader Peter and Dinah began to incorporate inlay on their fetishes. They were probably the first artists at Zuni to decorate their carvings with inlaid heartlines; they made these either as continuous lines, or with a gap in front of the animal's "mouth." In the 1960s, with Edna's encouragement, they made flat bird fetishes for stringing which they sold for a dollar apiece. Fortunately they became skilled enough to "make them pretty fast." For a while the couple made custom jewelry and worked for Joe Tanner doing inlay on Preston Monongye's tufa-cast silver pieces.

Early in their careers Peter and Dinah made bears, foxes, and wolves, and they became noted for their bug-eyed frogs. They preferred working in jet, amber, and serpentine. Together since about 1959, they continue to work as a team, making fetishes in their distinctive style. Their animals have always been very rounded and smooth, and their fine polishing has remained a special trademark. Recently they have begun "signing" fetishes with a stamped, circular, silver hallmark. Their children also pursue the art: Elroy, Peter, Jr., and Debra Gasper each work in a style that reflects the family tradition. Peter and Dinah's late son Braden was known for his howling coyotes, a subject now regularly copied at Zuni.

Dinah's sister, Lena Boone (1946–) worked in the office and in sales for the Zuni Craftsmen Cooperative Association in the late 1960s. She helped her mother make fetishes, just as she had helped her grandfather Teddy Weahkee late in his life, when her job was to drill shells for Teddy's notoriously fancy bundles.

Lena and Rignie Boone (1945–1984) were together before he began serving in the army in 1967. During his tour of duty in Vietnam, Rignie worked in communications, but when he returned to Zuni in 1971 he was unable to find work in that field. Instead he began helping his mother-in-law, Edna Leki, with her fetishes.

By 1972 Rignie and Lena were earning their living by carving. Besides Lena's heritage of talented ancestors, Rignie was the great-nephew of Leekya Deyuse. His grandfather was Leekya's brother Alec, who according to Lena, carved fetishes only occasionally but exhibited quality workmanship. Nevertheless Rignie and Lena's style was decidedly different from that of other family members. For example, the noses on their animals are more pointed. Rignie was the first to make hummingbird fetish necklaces, which many Zuni and Navajo artists have since copied. In addition, Rignie and Lena produced standing bear, wolf, and fox fetishes in what, for the time, was an impressive array of materials. Their first buyers, who included the Harringtons and traders Wanda Short and Ken Schooley, often provided them with unusual stones. Today Lena uses a wider and more interesting variety of materials than almost any other carver at Zuni.

Lena's children, Leland and Evalena Boone, represent the family's fourth generation of carvers, together with their Gasper cousins, and with Michael and Chase Weahkee, the sons of Dinah and Lena's brother, Anderson Weahkee, who is also a carver. Anderson's late son Clay carved as well. All have continued in the traditional mode of Teddy Weahkee. Dinah and Lena's sister, Sandra Gregory, also helped Edna and other family members complete their work. Because she has remained behind the scenes, Sandra has never received the recognition she deserves.

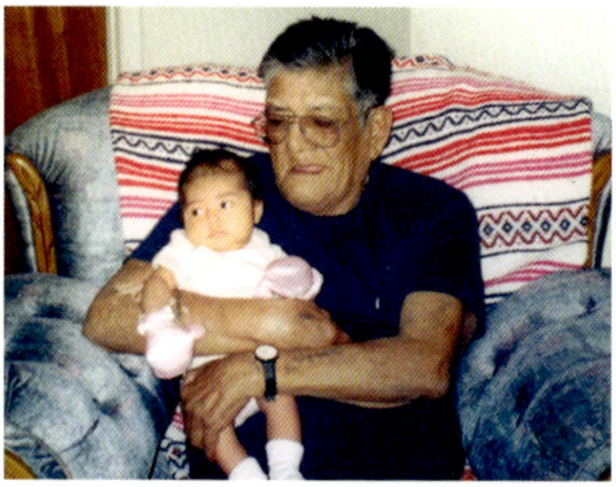

Bobby Lonasee holding granddaughter Aaliyah Little Bird, circa 2003. Collection of Bobby Lonasee.

BOBBY LONASEE

Known for his antler carvings, Bobby Lonasee (1932–2004) began making fetishes in the 1960s, after making cluster-style earrings and other jewelry for several years. He was highly productive in the 1970s and 1980s, and carved until 1993, when illness forced him to stop. In 2004, with his family's encouragement, he began again to do a small amount of carving, but he passed away in October of that year.

Bobby switched from making jewelry to carving fetishes largely because carving brought him a better income. He reported that he could earn eight to ten dollars for a standing fetish—good money for the time. He earned notoriety for frogs, hummingbirds, and his favorites, owls and turtles. Bobby occasionally worked in Ojo rock, an argillaceous stone found near Ojo Caliente, south of Zuni. But his favorite carving material was antler. Because deer and elk shed antler naturally, he could find it easily in the woods and incur no cash expense in obtaining it. He usually used deer antler, except when he made large fetishes for which elk antler was more suitable. Because antler gives off a strong odor when heated by carving, Bobby used his electric grinder out behind his home. He sometimes achieved contrast on his pieces by decorating them with inlaid dots of turquoise or jet. His early customers included Chet Jones and Greg Hofmann.

In addition to making jewelry and fetishes, Bobby farmed and raised sheep and horses, and was a smoke jumper working with hotshot firefighting crews in the Gila National Forest. Perhaps most importantly, Bobby was a spiritual man, deeply involved in the religious duties of Zuni. His passing was a great loss to the village.

Bobby lived surrounded by family, including his children Clifford, Andres, Florenda, Karen, Florine, Gloria, and Craig. Clifford, Florenda, and Andres continue the tradition of fetish carving, often using antler as their father did, and frequently carving the animals he liked in a style reminiscent of his.

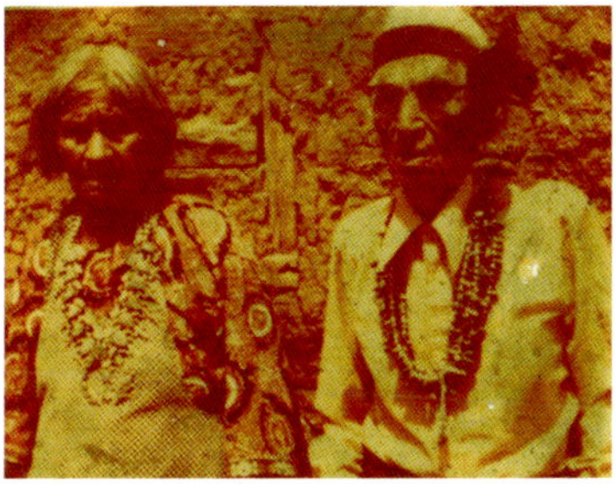

Edith and Sepo Ponchuella, circa 1975.
Collection of Lena Ponchuella.

SEPO PONCHUELLA

Sepo Ponchuella (1881–1978) was another carver of the older generation who remained active in the 1970s. In fact it is likely that he began carving in the 1960s, when he was more than eighty years old. Until that time Sepo specialized in cluster jewelry and single-row bracelets. He gave up the exacting work of making jewelry as his eyesight weakened.

Like many carvers of his generation, Sepo's tools included hand-cranked grinding wheels, hand-pumped drills, and files. He used an emery cloth to smooth his pieces, and he buffed them on his knee with a piece of leather to which he applied polishing powder. Sepo never used electric equipment. He even preferred to use a kerosene lamp at home, long after electricity had come to Zuni.

Sepo liked to carve local materials and was particularly fond of Ojo rock. He was known for his bears, which he often embellished with painted features. Sepo's great-granddaughter LoRae Lonasee remembers listening to stories that he told while he carved. He sold his work to several dealers, but his granddaughter Delia Ponchuella particularly remembers Leon Ingraham. In addition to carving, Sepo and his family were great sheepherders. Sepo's grandson Lawrence Lonasee remembers that they maintained as many as 1,000 sheep near the settlement of Ojo Caliente.

Sepo carved almost until the time of his death. While neither of his children, Leon Ponchuella and Rosalie Hoosewa, took up carving, several of his grandchildren and great-grandchildren have followed in his footsteps. These include Louise Wallace, Wilford and Faylena Cachini, and LoRae Lonasee. Several other family members continued his silversmithing tradition.

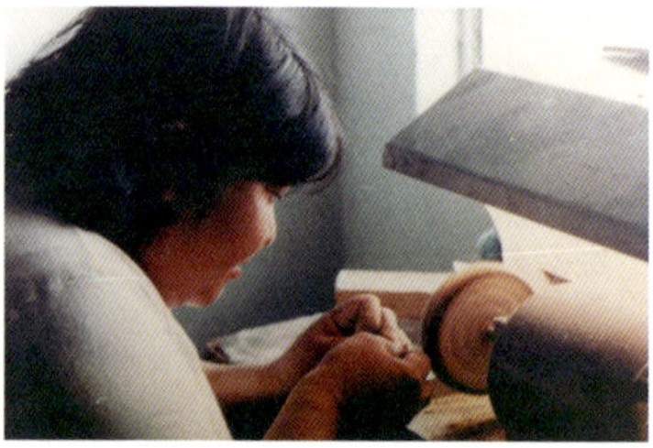

Rosalia Quam carving, circa 1975.
Collection of Georgette Quam.

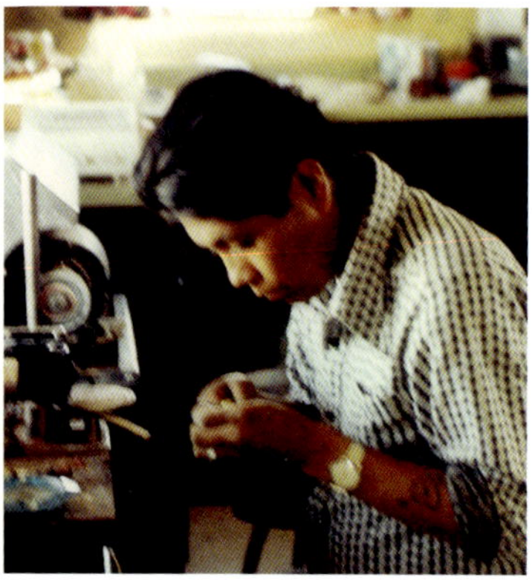

Andrew Emerson Quam carving, circa 1975.
Collection of Georgette Quam.

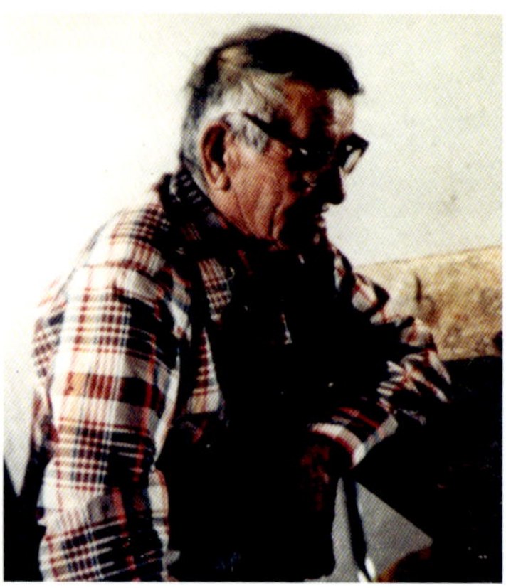

George Cheechee Haloo, circa 1975.
Collection of Georgette Quam.

ROSALIA AND ANDREW EMERSON QUAM

Rosalia Quam (1941–1989) was the step-daughter of George Cheechee Haloo (1908–1983), and wife of Andrew Emerson Quam (1943–1976), two of Zuni's most celebrated makers of fetish necklaces. George was a self-taught carver who began making fetishes in the 1930s. He inspired all of his children: Lita Delena, Miguel Haloo, Ramie Haloo, and Tina Sice, as well as Rosalia. Both Rosalia and Andrew Emerson began carving in the 1960s, and along with George became known for their bird fetishes. They used electric tools for carving, but early on drilled their stringing fetishes with a hand-pumped drill. Unlike most other carvers, neither they nor George ever made silver jewelry.

When Rosalia and Andrew Emerson separated in the mid-1970s, Rosalia reinvented her artistic career. She decided to stop making stringing fetishes and to concentrate solely on standing carvings which, according to her daughter Georgette Quam, Anderson never made. Rosalia created a wide variety of animals, including frogs, owls, horses, turtles, bears, and squirrels. While her frogs were decidedly bulbous, her other animals were often sharply angular. Her favorite media were shell, turquoise, and serpentine. She sold her work to the Harringtons and to Leon Ingraham, among others.

Rosalia and Andrew Emerson both carved until shortly before their deaths. Today all of their children carve, including Andrew, Georgette, Eldred, Andres, Prudencia, Dwight, and Tyler Quam; and they in turn have taught spouses, relatives, and friends. In fact, this branch of the Quam family has probably produced and influenced more carvers than any other family in Zuni. The Quams create fetishes in a variety of styles from simple to naturalistic, and their work, like that of their parents, remains very popular.

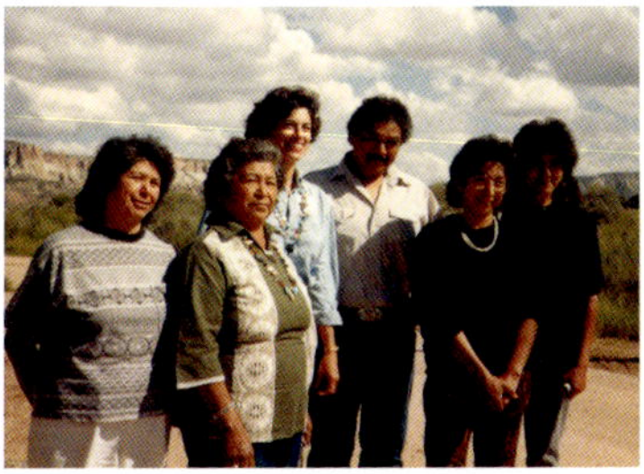

Albenita Yunie, Ellen Quandelacy, an unidentified woman, Stewart Quandelacy, Faye Quandelacy, and Georgia Quandelacy, circa 1990. Collection of Stewart Quandelacy.

THE QUANDELACY FAMILY

One of the most important carving families in Zuni, the Quandelacys are responsible for initiating or at least popularizing a number of innovations in the art of fetish making. Most of the Quandelacys started carving as children, out of necessity. Sandra Quandelacy remembers that they were very poor, and that feeding their large family was difficult. She remembers that in the 1960s, the children augmented the family income by making and selling antler owls. Her brother Stewart recalls that the children carved prairie dogs of antler, which they attached to abalone shell bases; and that they made antler creatures dubbed "ugly monsters" by trader John Kennedy. According to Stewart, they also made copper jewelry and small beaded dolls, but neither of these activities was as lucrative as making fetishes, for which Kennedy and Tobe Turpen paid $1.50 to $2.00 apiece. Wilmer, Stewart, and Dickie, the first of the Quandelacy children to carve, started while they were in grade school in the small Zuni reservation community of Pescado. They used hand-cranked grinding wheels to form their creations, one child holding the fetish against the wheel as another turned the crank.

The Quandelacy children took inspiration from their parents, Ellen (1924–2002), and Dixie (1908–1979), both of whom worked primarily as jewelers. Ellen, who was best known for channel-inlaid jewelry, was nevertheless the first in the immediate family to carve. She occasionally made "concretion-style" fetishes, on which only minimal carving is done to enhance the natural shape of the stone. Ellen made few fetishes until around 1990, when a stroke made it difficult for her to hold the soldering torch she used as a jeweler. As a fetish carver, she became known for her old-style, flat-sided horses.

As an adult Dickie became a jeweler who produced beautiful inlay and who carved sandstone fetishes only occasionally. Wilmer has never carved frequently, and rarely makes fetishes today. However Stewart (1949–) became a full-time carver. He served in the Navy in Vietnam from 1968 to 1972. Upon his discharge he worked in construction, and for a brief period attended school part-time. By 1974 he was carving on a regular basis, in part because it was a familiar occupation, but also because he had little money to invest, and carving materials were less expensive than silver and turquoise. At first he made stringing fetishes—primarily birds and bears—but standing fetishes soon followed. He did inlay work on most of his fetishes, often adding a heartline that ended in a circle rather than the arrow shape he later adopted. Sometime in the 1970s Stewart originated the "medicine bear" with its famous lightning-shaped heartline. He attributes the idea to paintings he had seen on Zuni Medicine Society altars. To this day Stewart strives "to give each piece character." As children the Quandelacys tried to make their animals "look real," and according to Stewart the family has continued to work in a realistic style. He says the family's many artistic innovations have come about naturally because "they appeal to the eye."

Andres Quandelacy (1962–) started carving fetishes while in high school, at first specializing in buffalo. He says he was the first to make fish-carrying bears, the first to make textured bears, and the first to make standing bears (although this innovation is also claimed by at least one other family). These accomplishments make Andres one of Zuni's most influential carvers. Like Stewart, he wanted his first animals to "look like what they were," and so took a realistic approach to carving. He confesses that he never concentrated on making jewelry because he "couldn't get the hang of it." Early in high school he sold fetishes to Zuni trader Benjamin Tzuni and to the Harringtons. Andres served in the Marines from 1981 to 1984.

Faye Quandelacy (1958–) started carving in 1966 at the age of eight. She says that her father, Dixie Quandelacy, was her inspiration. Although he was primarily a jeweler, Dixie sometimes carved antler serpents, and once made a Corn

Maiden figurine out of the end of an antler. Faye pursued the idea, and made the first of her famous Corn Maidens in the 1970s. From 1979 to 1982 Faye attended the Institute of American Indian Arts (IAIA) in Santa Fe, where she studied sculpture. Stewart says her sculpting influenced him to do larger, more sculptural pieces as well.

As a child Sandra Quandelacy watched her mother Ellen make jewelry. She experimented with the craft while she was in college, and ultimately focused seriously on it. She occasionally carved fetishes as well, but only began carving full-time during the 1990s. Today she, like Faye, is known for elegant Corn Maidens.

Starting in the late 1970s, Barlow Quandelacy (1960–1992) made fetishes with textured surfaces and heartlines, as well as standing and fish-carrying bears. Albenita Yunie worked in the post office in Robert Wallace's trading post until her sister Georgia encouraged her to start carving fetishes. Georgia herself began in the 1980s, as did their brother Avery.

The family has remained modest about their influence on Zuni fetish carving. Although their fetishes exhibit refinement and aesthetic quality, Sandra doesn't think of them as "art." But trendsetters they have been, and many stylistic traits and types of fetishes found at Zuni today originated with the Quandelacys. The children of Albenita, Stewart, Dickie, Georgia, and Faye also carve, thus insuring that the family legacy will endure.

Annie Gasper Quam (1926–2001), the sister of Ellen Quandelacy, made fetishes as early as the 1950s, although she did not carve regularly until the 1990s. Her children Phillip Pinto (1950–1977), Lynn Quam, Rhoda Quam, and Pernell Gasper (1962–1984), all began making stringing fetishes in the 1970s. Today Lynn and Rhoda make standing fetishes. Lynn began carving them in about 1980 along with his wife Jayne, a Navajo from Utah. According to Lynn, Phillip made only stringing fetishes, but Pernell made both stringing and standing carvings. This branch of the family sold their work to trader Jeff Lewis and to Greg Hofmann of Turquoise Village, but early examples are hard to find.

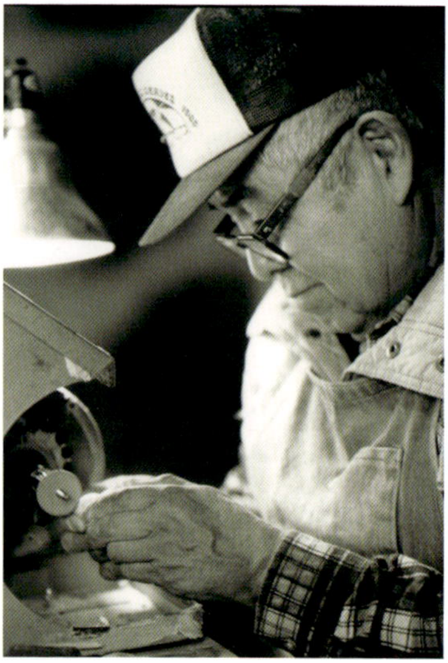

Aaron Sheche carving, circa 1990. Photograph © Joel Gordon. Collection of Thelma and Lorandina Sheche.

AARON AND THELMA SHECHE

Aaron Sheche (1915–2002) had a gift common to many great sculptors. A man who served with Aaron in the Army Air Force during World War II observed it first-hand. He recalled that when they were together in Italy in about 1942, Aaron would pick up a rock and say, "I see a bear in that rock," or "there's a mountain lion in there." It left a lasting impression on Aaron's friend, who told the story to Pat Harrington 40 years later.

Aaron began his creative career making inlaid bracelets and chokers. In 1948 he married Thelma (1928–), daughter of the great traditional carver Theodore Kucate. The couple noticed that as Theodore aged he used his tools less often. According to Thelma, she and Aaron didn't like to see them lying around untouched, so they picked them up and began putting them to work. By the 1960s Aaron had branched out into carving, and by 1972 he and Thelma were producing fetishes in earnest. They sold most of their early work to Tobe Turpen, the Harringtons, and trader and author Oscar Branson.

Aaron tried a little bit of everything. His early works recalled Theodore's traditional style, similar to the fetishes illustrated in Frank Hamilton Cushing's "Zuni Fetiches." However by the mid-1970s Aaron's fetishes were more naturalistic and included rams, horses, turtles, human figures, bears, and a variety of birds, among others. Aaron's family recalls that he was single-minded about his carving, and even when he had orders to fill, worked most of the time on what pleased him. Eventually traders encouraged Aaron to return to the older style, which hampered the expression of his inventive talent, but it made it possible for Thelma and him to complete fetishes quickly and more easily, and to meet the demand for their work. Aaron's family believes that his independent nature contributed to the endurance of his legacy.

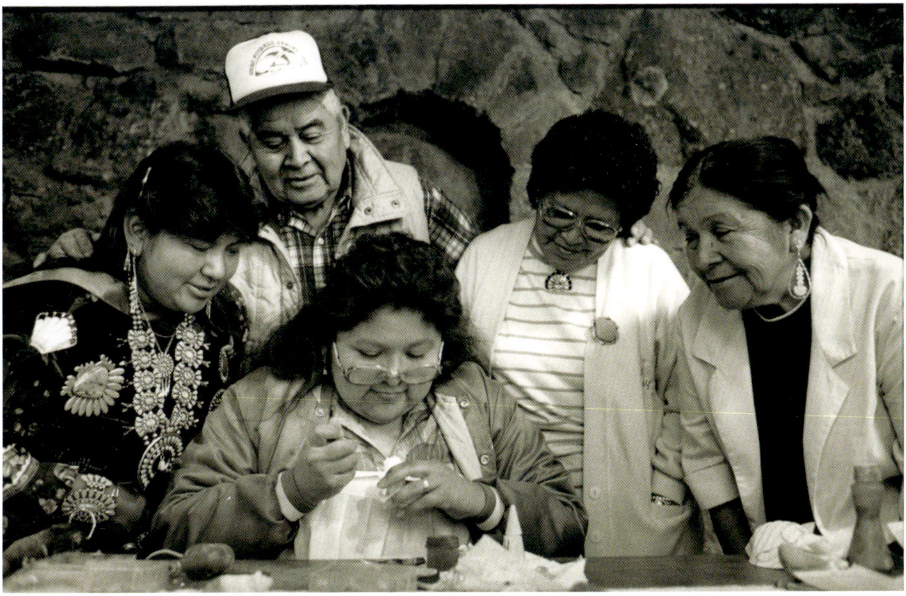

Karen Ykestine, Aaron Sheche, Lorandina Sheche, Arless Luna, and Thelma Sheche at the Museum of Northern Arizona, circa 1990. Photograph © Joel Gordon. Collection of Thelma and Lorandina Sheche.

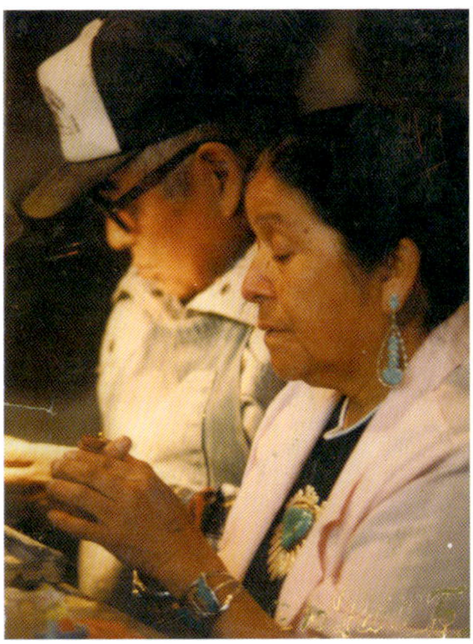

Aaron and Thelma Sheche working on fetishes, circa 1990. Collection of Thelma and Lorandina Sheche.

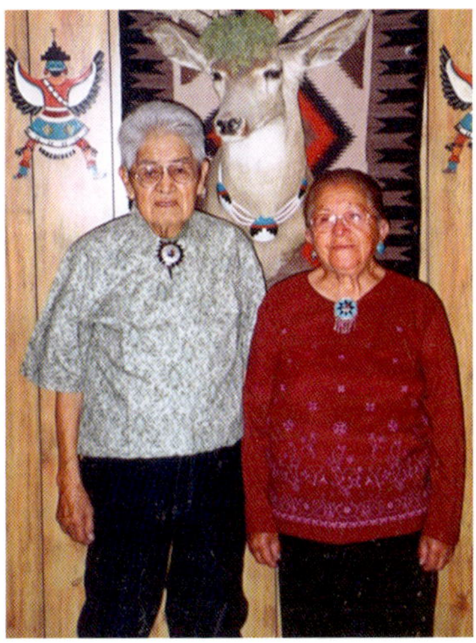

Aaron and Thelma Sheche at home, circa 2000. Collection of Thelma and Lorandina Sheche.

In addition to carving, Aaron herded sheep and held the important job of fire crew boss. Theodore Kucate had started a dance troupe with Aaron, Thelma, and five of their children. Following Theodore's death, Aaron kept the troupe going until the mid-1980s.

By 1980, Aaron and Thelma's daughter Lorandina Sheche had embraced the family's art. She began by helping to make their popular male and female coyote sets: Aaron roughed out the fetishes, Thelma "refined" them, and Lorandina polished them and added their distinctive bundles. Today Lorandina continues to carve fetishes, as do Aaron and Thelma's grandchildren, Aaron Chapella and Marnella and Trilisha Kucate. Arden Kucate, an infrequent carver, sits on the Zuni Tribal Council. The family's fourth generation of carvers proudly maintains Theodore Kucate's traditional style.

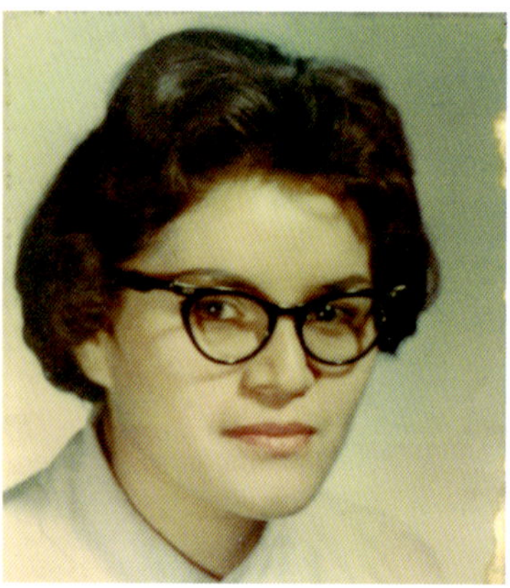

Lavina Kaskalla, high school photograph, circa 1957. Collection of Leonard and Lavina Kaskalla.

MARY TSIKEWA, BILL TSIKEWA, LEONARD AND LAVINA KASKALLA, RUDOLPH TSIKEWA, AND DAVID TSIKEWA, JR.

The daughter of Teddy Weahkee, sister of Edna Leki, and wife of David Tsikewa, Mary Tsikewa (1919–1986) spent her life surrounded by a wealth of talent. She began her own carving career in the 1950s. While her work was in some ways similar to her husband's, her carvings were simpler and more angular. She and David produced a variety of animals, but Mary was especially known for the birds she made for stringing. Mary also carved a variety of standing fetishes, including wolves, frogs, and turtles, and her signature livestock fetishes, which included horses, goats, and rams. She enjoyed using many kinds of serpentine as well as shell and turquoise. Mary sold her work to several traders including Joe Tanner.

David and Mary had eight children including Bill, Delano, Lavina, Jennie, Rudolph (1947–1991), David Jr. (1949–1975), Marvin, and Annette. It is possible that they all carved stringing fetishes, although Delano's history is unclear.

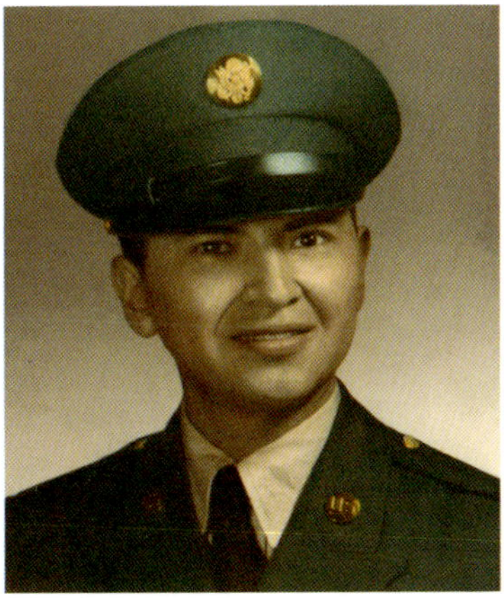

Leonard Kaskalla, Fort Carson, Colorado, circa 1962. Collection of Leonard and Lavina Kaskalla.

Rudolph, David Jr., Jennie, and Annette all started carving stringing fetishes in the 1970s; Marvin started later. Bill and Annette earned recognition primarily for their standing pieces.

Bill Tsikewa (1935–) became a silversmith while in high school, and began making fetish necklaces in the early 1970s. But he soon switched to making standing fetishes, especially bears and rams. Following his mother's example, he sold his early work to Joe Tanner.

Bill has had careers outside the arts as well. He served in the Navy from 1955 to 1959, and then in law enforcement, including work with the Gallup and the Bureau of Indian Affairs police departments. He is a former Chief Judge and has been Police Commissioner at Zuni, and at this writing he is in his second term on the Zuni Tribal Council.

Lavina Kaskalla (1938–) was the first of her generation to carve, starting in around 1970 with her husband Leonard (1938–), about the time her father David passed away. Prior to that, Leonard served in the Army from 1962 to 1964, and the couple produced channel-inlaid jewelry together. Lavina has always enjoyed making stringing fetishes, including birds, bears, foxes, wolves, and mountain lions. Leonard's first standing fetishes included horses, bears, foxes, and mountain lions. In their early work both Lavina and Leonard used serpentine, shell, and pipestone. They sold most of their early fetishes to the Harringtons, trader Gary Zens, and Turquoise Village. Like other contemporary carvers, they use electric tools. Lavina used to provide loose fetishes for traders to string, but today she makes her own necklaces, to which she attaches a signature tag. She began signing her necklaces because they have been misidentified in several books as the work of other artists.

Leonard and Lavina have been together since 1967 and have three children—Duran, Vaughn, and David Kaskalla. Duran and David make fetishes infrequently, and Vaughn is just beginning to carve.

While the children of David and Mary Tsikewa are known for their strung birds and bears, each member works in a slightly different style. The differences are subtle, and not always easy for the untrained eye to identify.

CONCLUSION

A time of popular success (and sometimes artistic excess), the 1970s both helped and hurt the development and quality of Native American art. While talented new artists rose to prominence, others became mass production workers, repeating the same designs over and over to ensure their economic security. Jewelry took center stage and temporarily overshadowed other traditional arts.

Nevertheless, Native American art survived. Promising and innovative new potters, weavers, and katsina doll carvers emerged, and Zuni Pueblo advanced its own fresh cadre of fetish carvers. Some created sleek, highly polished figures that suggested modern art. Others presented simpler work in the traditional style of their forefathers. And a few offered fanciful pieces that bordered on folk art. When we consider the limited array of carving materials available at the time, the depth of their production is amazing. Imagine these same artists working with today's vast lapidary palette.

During the 1970s Zuni craftswomen came to the forefront beginning with Edna Leki and including Lena Boone, Dinah Gasper, Alice Homer, Lavina Kaskalla, Sadie Laahty, Sarah Leekya, Marvelita Phillips, Rosalia Quam, Ellen and Faye Quandelacy, Thelma Sheche, and Mary Tsikewa. All paved the way for today's female carvers, opening the door to an art form previously dominated by men.

Most importantly, around forty tenacious artists kept fetish making alive and vital during a difficult period when it might have disappeared altogether. We owe the fetish carvers of the 1970s a debt of gratitude, and are pleased to offer this long-overdue tribute.

Elahkwa.

NOTES

1. Because there was another Deyuse family at Zuni (and even another Sarah), and because this resulted in confusion among governmental agencies, Leekya Deyuse's descendants adopted "Leekya" as their surname.

Zuni Fetish Carvers of the 1970s

A BRIDGE FROM PAST TO PRESENT

Old Man Acque

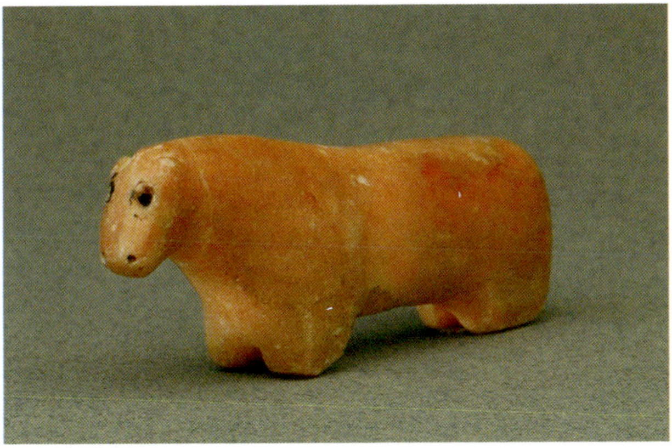

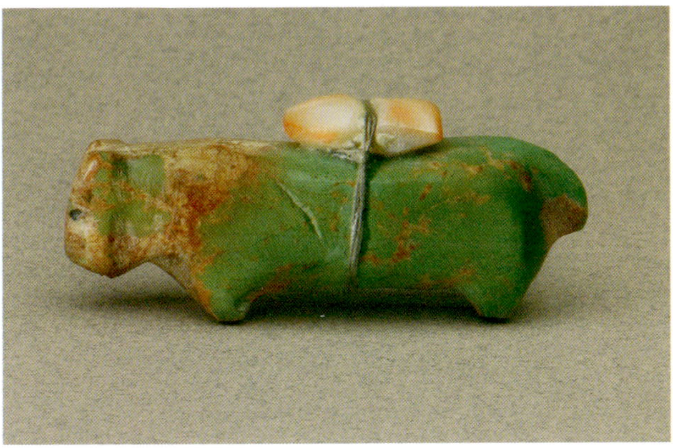

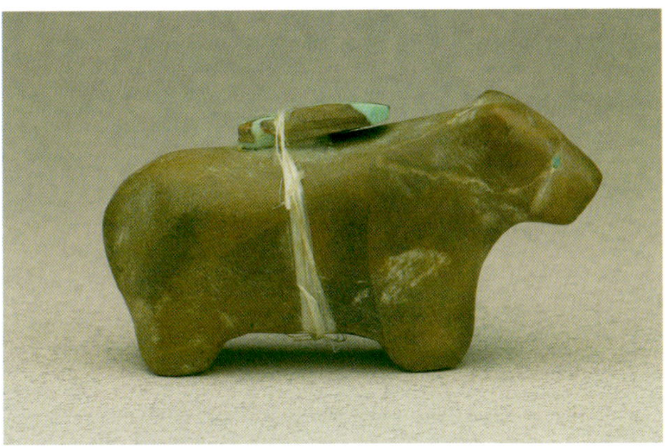

1. Orange alabaster horse. Length 2½ inches. Collection of Grey Dog Trading Company.

2. Turquoise horse. Length 2½ inches. Collection of Roger and Mary Crabtree.

3. Travertine bear. Length 2 inches. Private collection.

4. Left: turquoise bear. Length 4 inches. Collection of Roger and Mary Crabtree. Right: jasper bear. Length $2^1/_2$ inches. Private collection.

5. Serpentine bear. Length $3^5/_8$ inches. Collection of Challis L. Thiessen.

6. Purple stone wolf or coyote. Length $2\,^1/_4$ inches. Collection of Roger and Mary Crabtree.

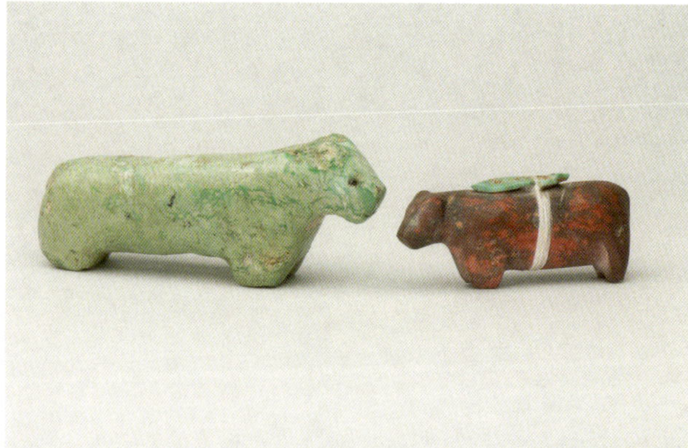

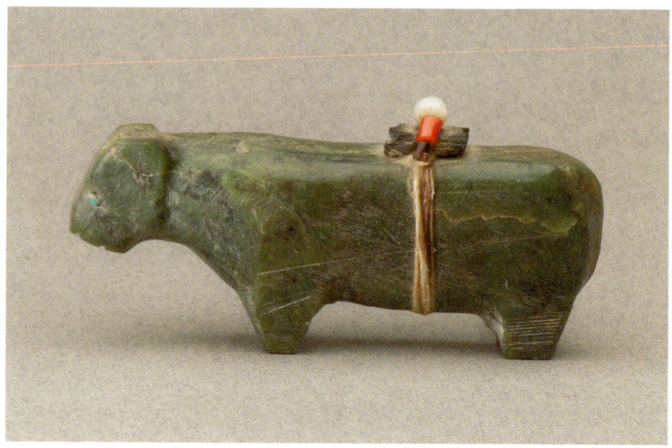

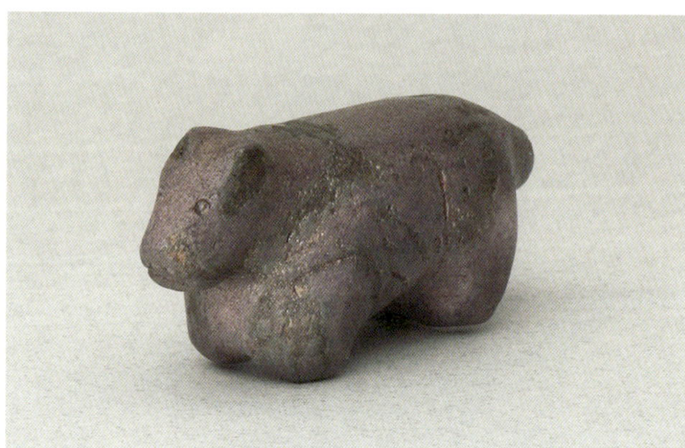

Harvey Bewanika

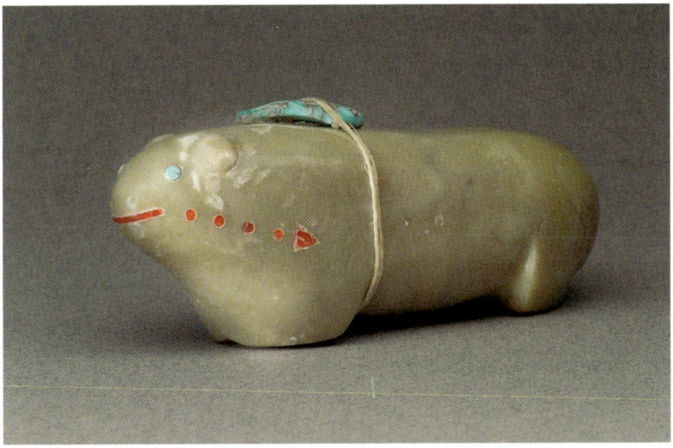

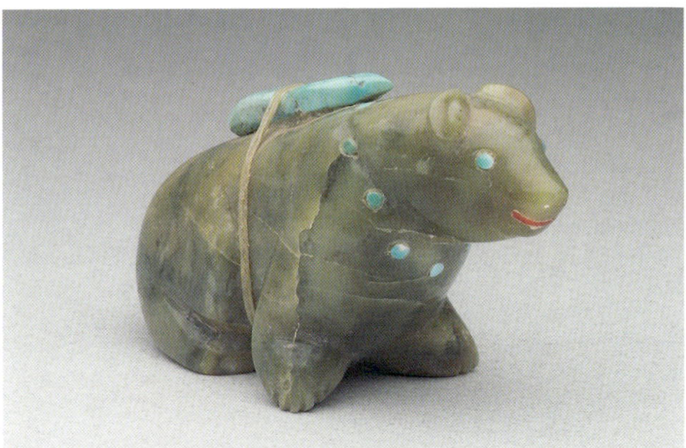

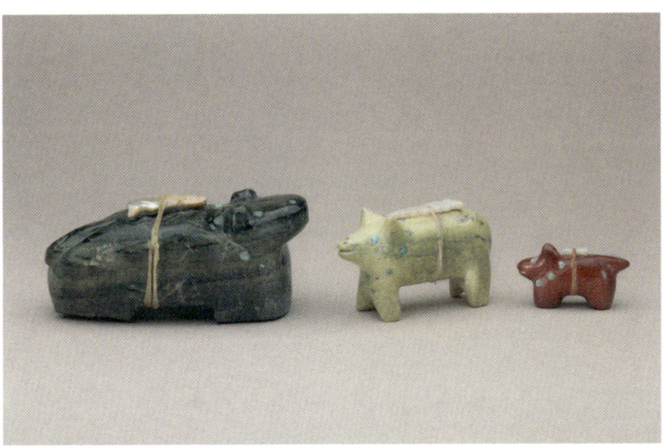

1. Serpentine bear with heartline of inlaid coral dots. Length 4 1/8 inches. Private collection.

2. Serpentine sitting bear with necklace of inlaid turquoise dots and inlaid coral mouth. Length 3 1/2 inches. Collection of Grey Dog Trading Company.

3. Left: serpentine bear with necklace of inlaid turquoise dots. Length 4 inches. Private collection. Center: serpentine bear with necklace of inlaid turquoise dots. Length 2 1/2 inches. Collection of Grey Dog Trading Company. Right: pipestone wolf or coyote with necklace of inlaid turquoise dots. Length 1 5/8 inches. Collection of Greg Hofmann, Turquoise Village.

4. Antler fox with inlaid turquoise dots. Length 4 1/4 inches. Private collection.

5. Serpentine sitting ram with necklace of inlaid turquoise dots and inlaid coral mouth. Length 3 inches. Private collection.

6. Left: serpentine frog with inlaid coral mouth. Length 2 3/8 inches. Collection of Challis L. Thiessen. Right: Nutria travertine frog. Length 1 3/4 inches. Private collection.

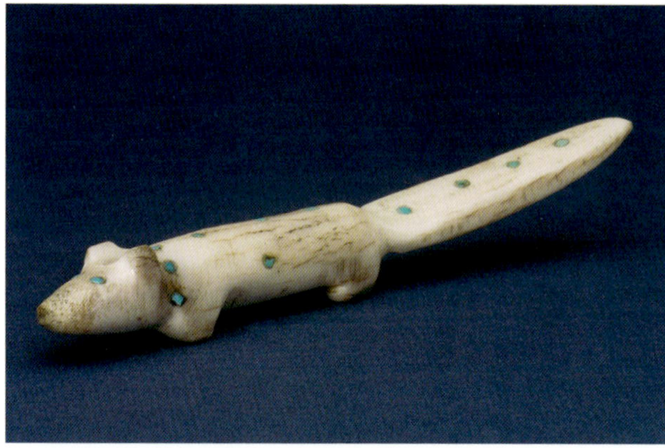

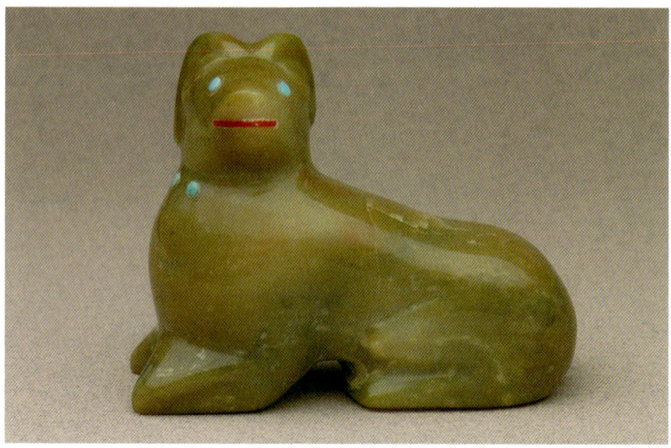

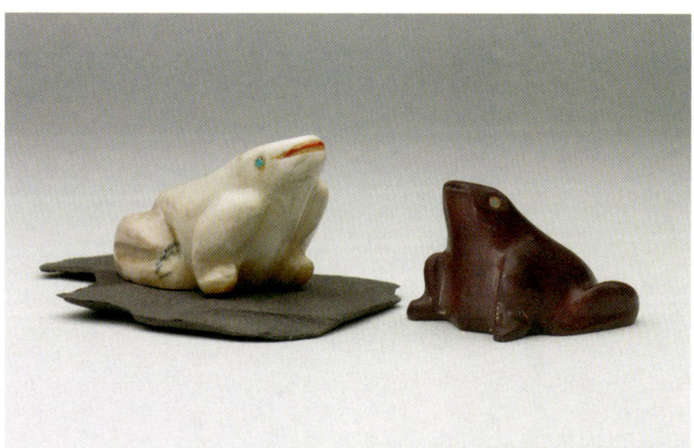

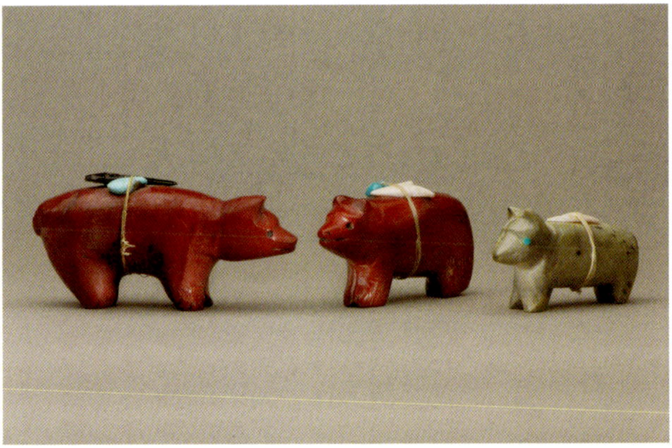

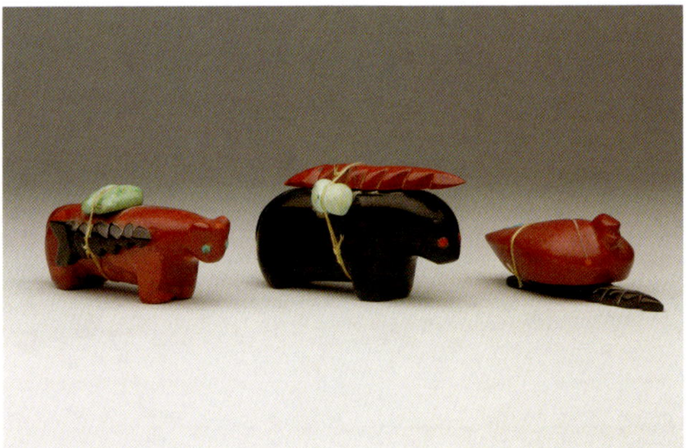

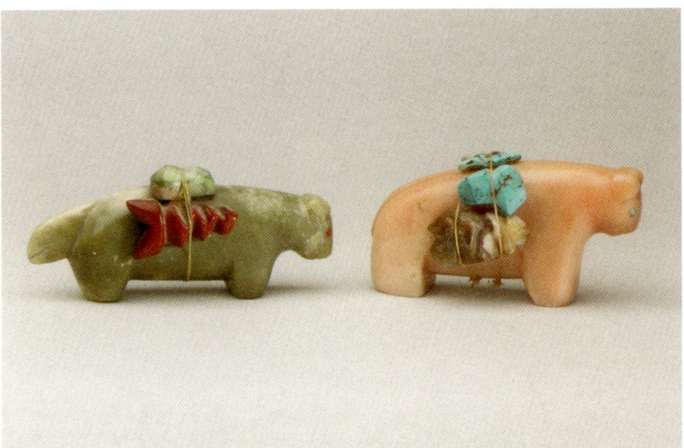

7. Left: pipestone bear. Length 3¾ inches. Private collection. Center: pipestone bear. Length 2⅞ inches. Collection of Christopher Rex. Right: serpentine bear. Length 2⅜ inches. Private collection.

8. Left: pipestone badger. Length 3 inches. Center: jet mole. Length 3 inches. Right: pipestone eagle. Length 3 inches. Private collections.

9. Left: serpentine wolf. Length 3⅜ inches. Private collection. Right: marble mountain lion. Length: 3⅛ inches. Collection of Greg Hofmann, Turquoise Village.

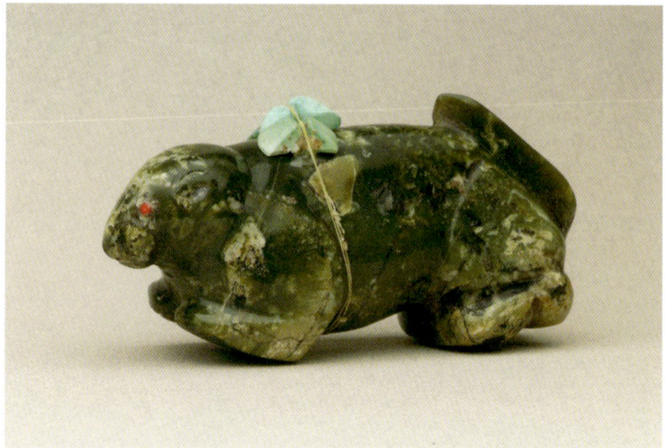

10. Serpentine mountain lion. Length 5 inches. Private collection.

Saul Yuselew

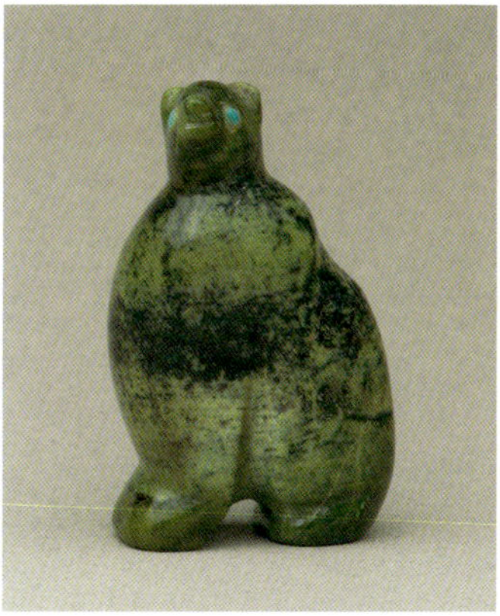

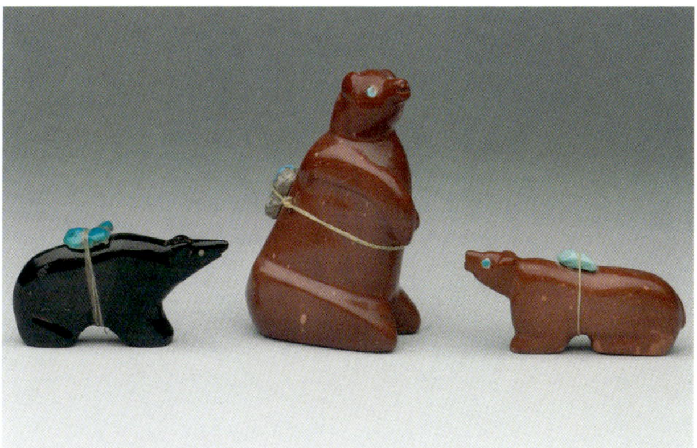

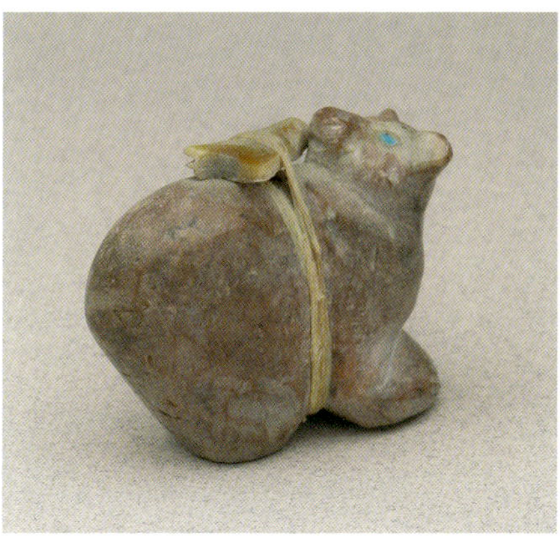

1. Serpentine sitting bear. Height 2¾ inches. Collection of Grey Dog Trading Company.

2. Left: jet bear. Length 2¼ inches. Collection of Grey Dog Trading Company. Center: pipestone sitting bear. Height 3 inches. Private collection. Right: pipestone bear. Length 2¼ inches. Collection of Roger and Mary Crabtree.

3. Serpentine bear. Length 1¾ inches. Private collection.

4. Serpentine frog. Length 2 inches. Private collection.

5. Left: serpentine mountain lion. Length 3 5/8 inches. Right: serpentine mountain lion. Length 2 1/4 inches. Private collection.

6. Mother-of-pearl bird. Length 3 inches. Private collection.

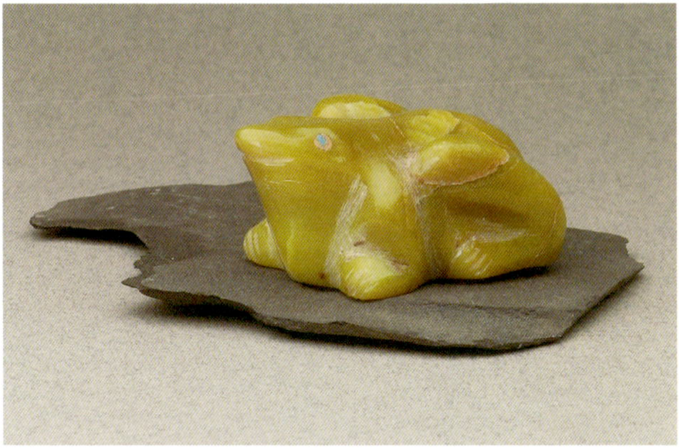

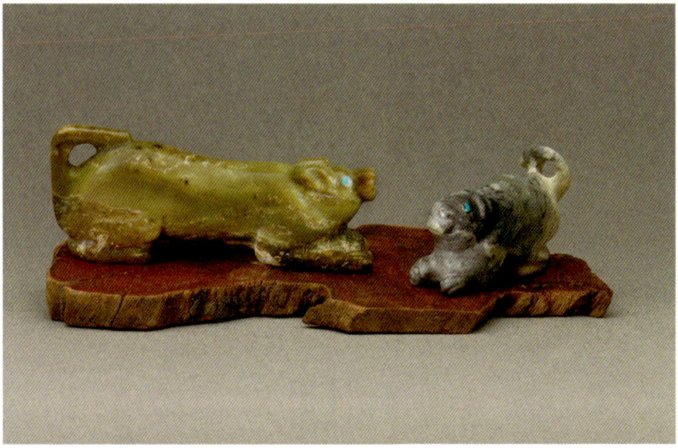

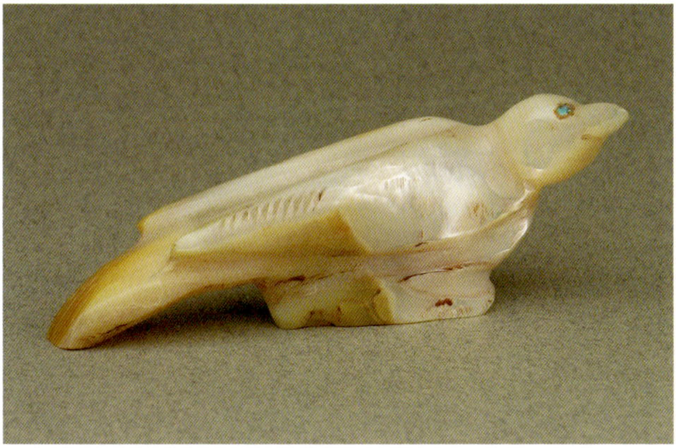

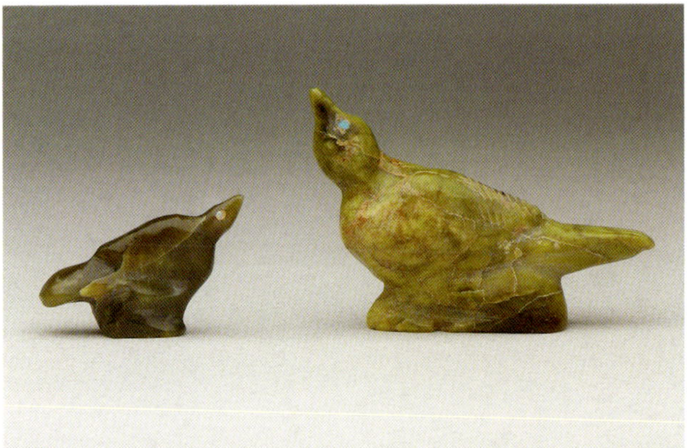

7. Left: serpentine bird.
Length 1½ inches.
Right: serpentine bird.
Length 2½ inches.
Private collections.

Leonard Halate

1. Left: travertine bear with inlaid coral heartline. Length 2⅜ inches. Right: serpentine bear with inlaid coral heartline. Length 2⅞ inches. Private collections.

2. Left: serpentine ram. Length 3⅝ inches. Right: orange alabaster ram. Length 2⅞ inches. Collection of J. Claire Dean.

3. Left: serpentine mountain lion. Length 2⅞ inches. Collection of Christopher Rex. Right: serpentine wolf. Length 3 inches. Collection of J. Claire Dean.

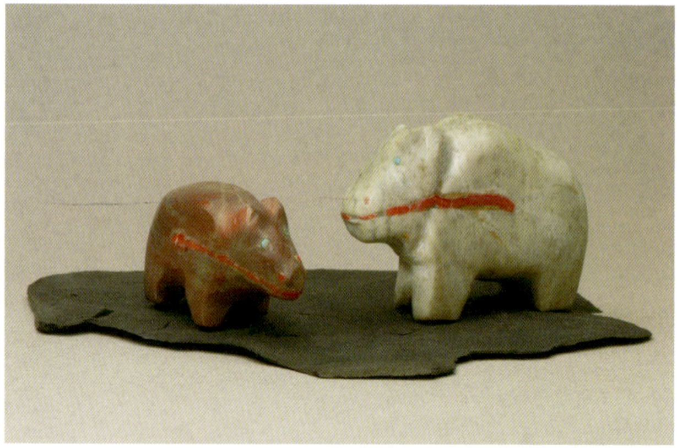

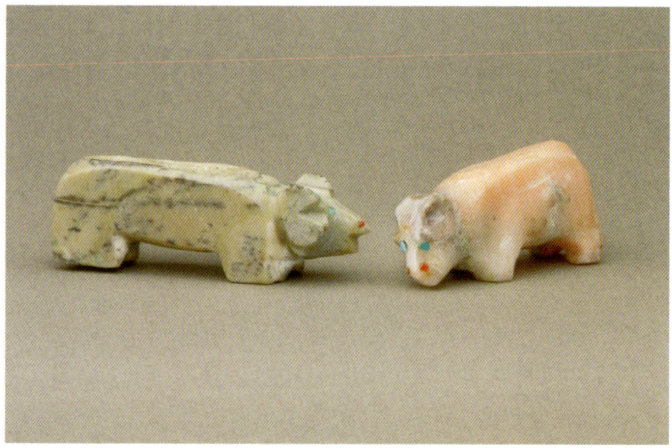

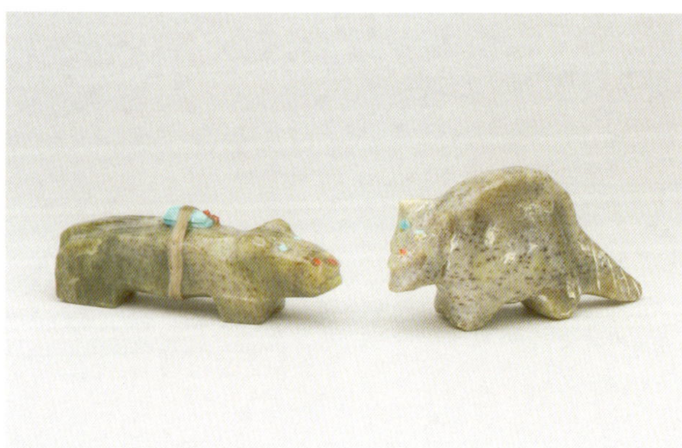

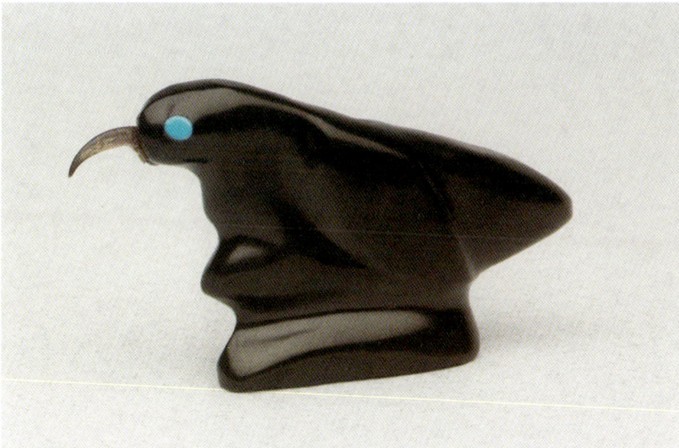

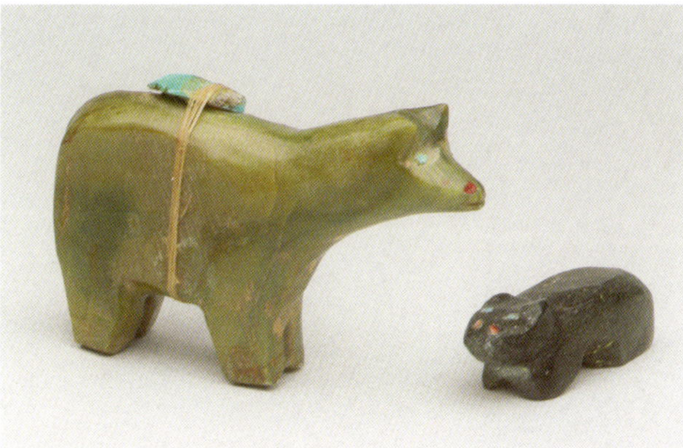

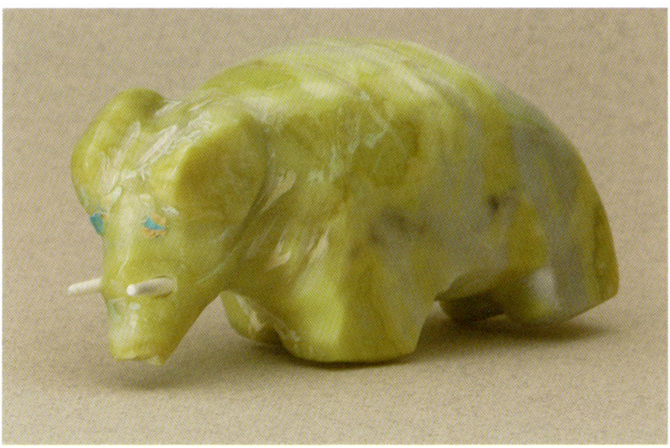

4. Jet bird. Length $2\frac{1}{8}$ inches. Collection of Greg Hofmann, Turquoise Village.

5. Left: serpentine animal. Length $3\frac{7}{8}$ inches. Collection of Challis L. Thiessen. Right: serpentine bear. Length 2 inches. Collection of Christopher Rex.

6. Serpentine elephant. Length $3\frac{1}{8}$ inches. Collection of J. Claire Dean.

Patrick and Marvelita Phillips

1. Antler water serpent by Patrick Phillips. Length 11¼ inches. Private collection.

2. Left: antler bear by Marvelita Phillips. Length 2⅞ inches. Collection of Christopher Rex. Center: alabaster bear by Marvelita Phillips. Length 2⅜ inches. Collection of Christopher Rex. Right: pipestone bear by Marvelita Phillips. Length 2⅛ inches. Private collection.

3. Left: antler "altar doll" by Marvelita Phillips. Height 3 inches. Private collection.

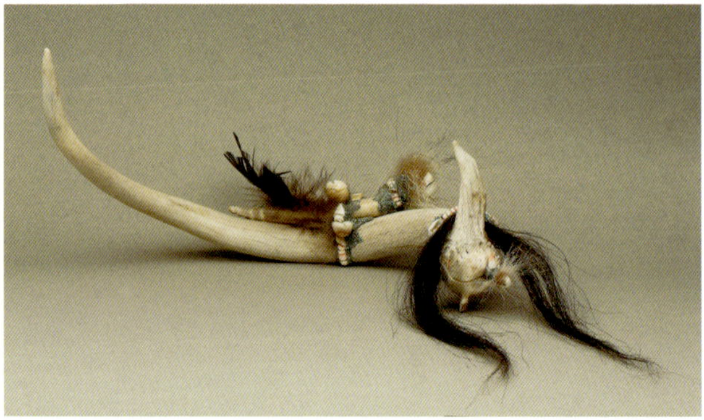

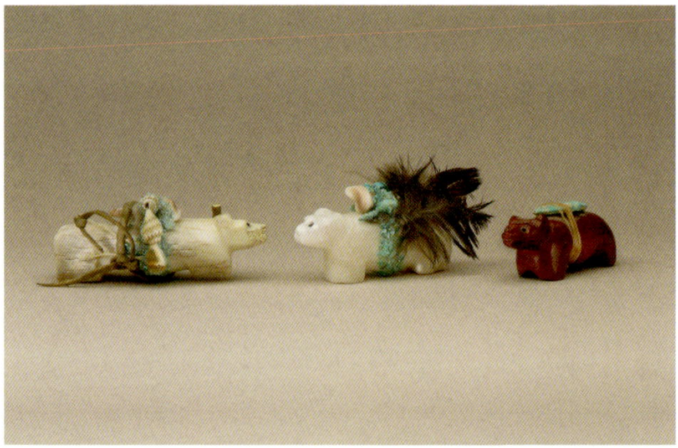

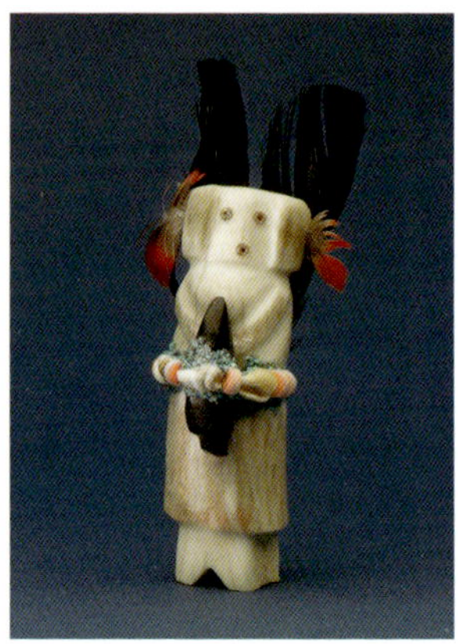

Alice Homer

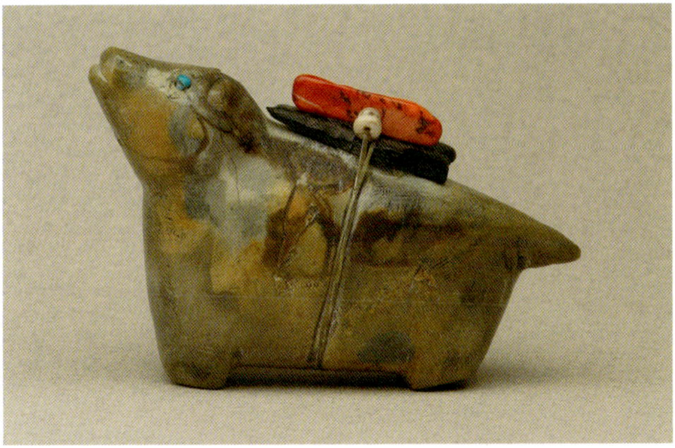

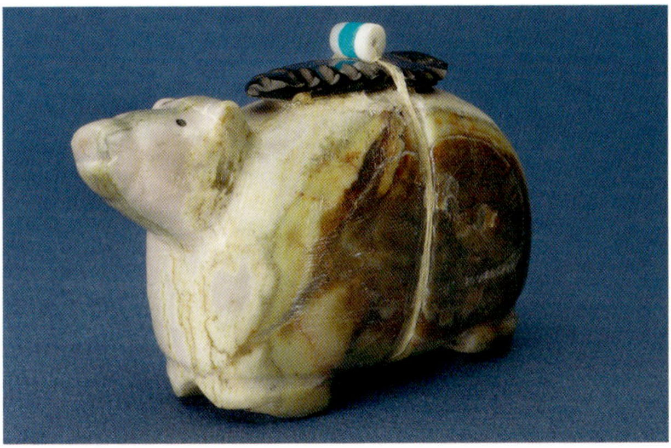

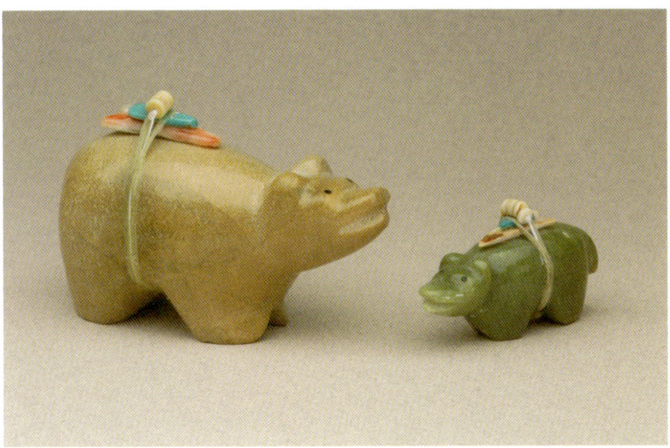

1. Zuni rock bear. Length 3 ¼ inches. Private collection.

2. Serpentine bear. Length 3 ⅜ inches. Private collection.

3. Left: Zuni rock bear. Length 3 ⅝ inches. Collection of Roger and Mary Crabtree. Right: serpentine bear. Length 2 ⅜ inches. Collection of Challis L. Thiessen.

4. Zuni rock wolf. Length 5¼ inches. Private collection.

5. Left: Zuni rock wolf. Length 4¾ inches. Right: serpentine wolf. Length 4⅞ inches. Collection of Challis L. Thiessen.

6. Left: serpentine wolf. Length 3¾ inches. Collection of Christopher Rex. Center: serpentine wolf. Length 4½ inches. Collection of Greg Hofmann, Turquoise Village. Right: travertine wolf. Length 3¼ inches. Private collection.

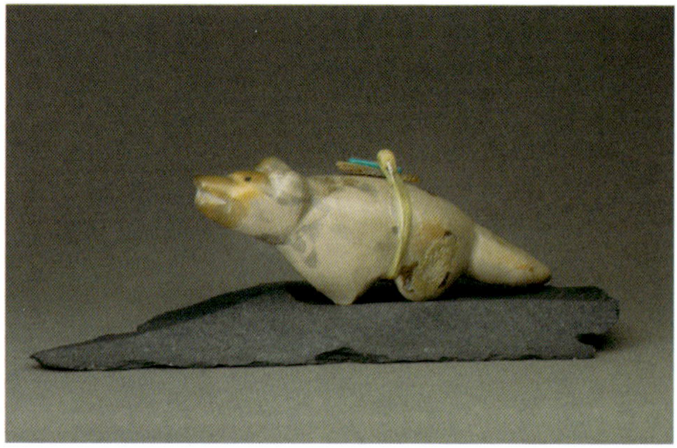

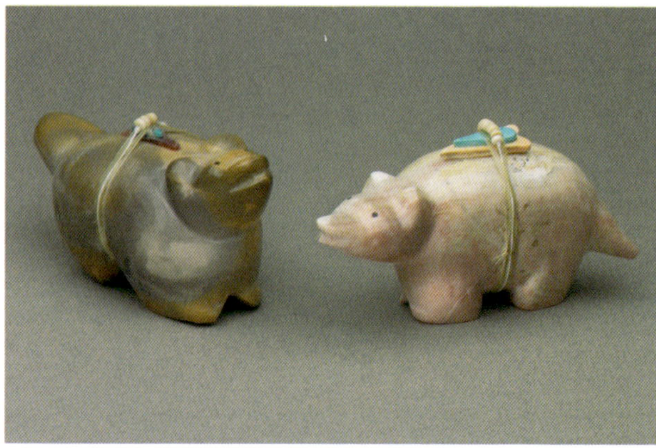

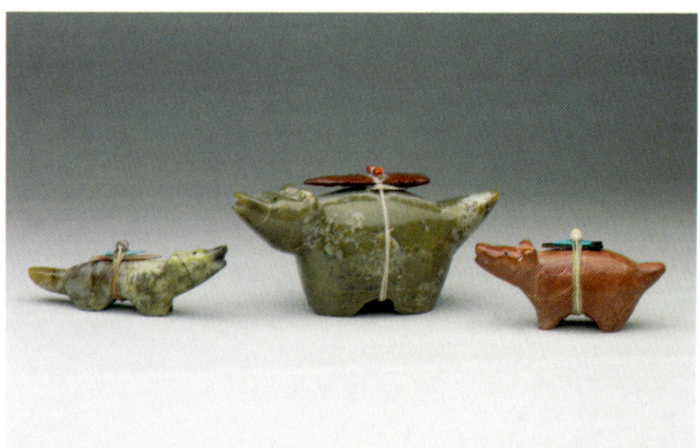

Bernard Homer, Jr.

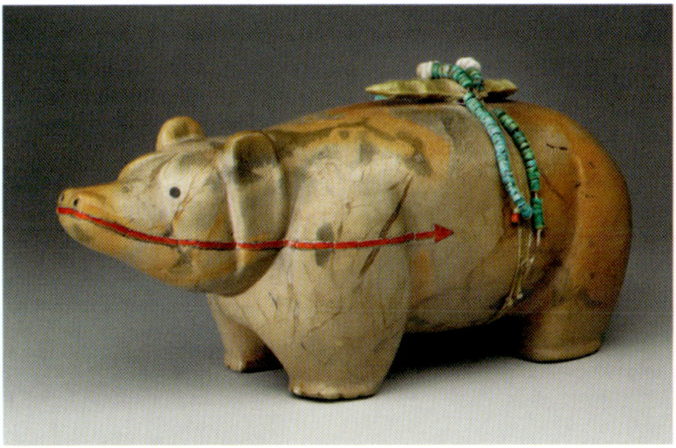

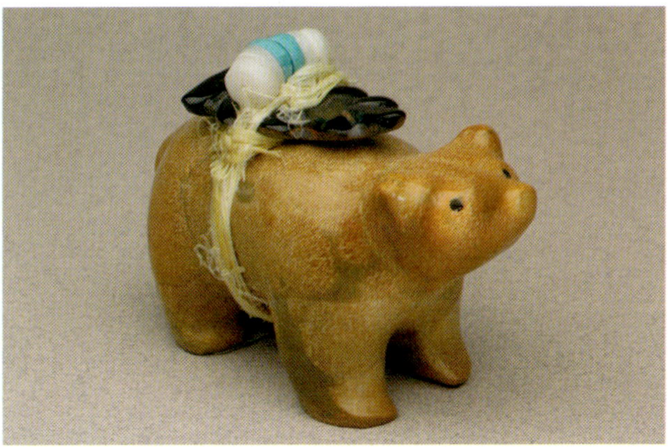

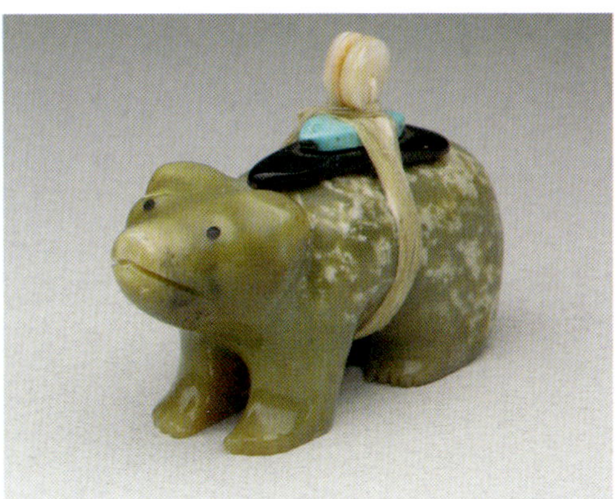

1. Zuni rock bear. Length 12½ inches. Collection of Joe and Cindy Tanner, Tanner's Indian Arts, Gallup, New Mexico. This piece was a blue-ribbon winner at Gallup Inter-Tribal Indian Ceremonial in 1968.

2. Zuni rock bear. Length 3⅜ inches. Collection of Andrews Pueblo Pottery.

3. Serpentine bear. Length 3⅜ inches. Collection of Christopher Rex.

4. Zuni rock wolf. Length 4½ inches. Private collection.

5. Green sea snail shell wolf pendant. Length 2¼ inches. Private collection.

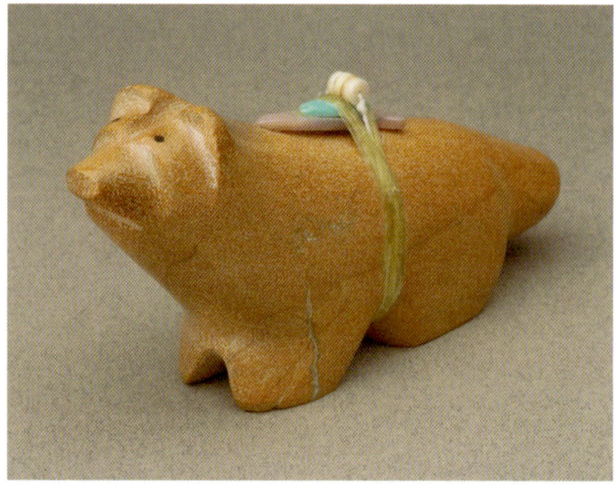

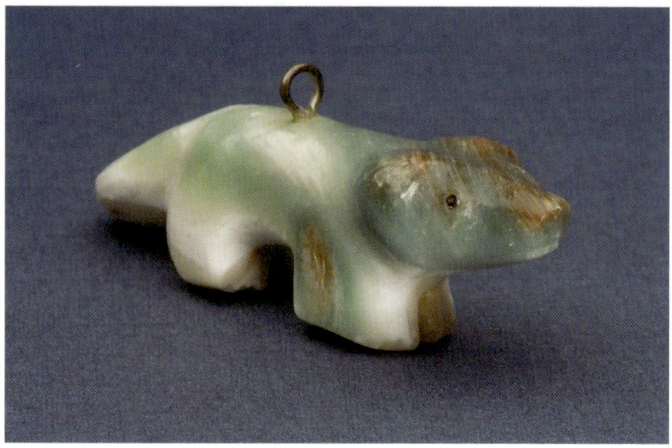

Sarah Leekya

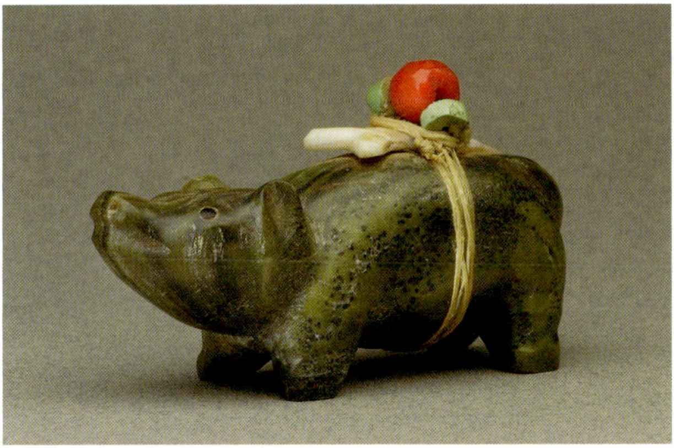

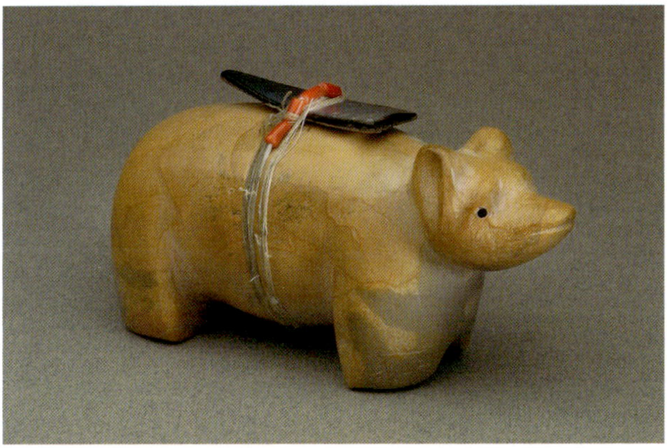

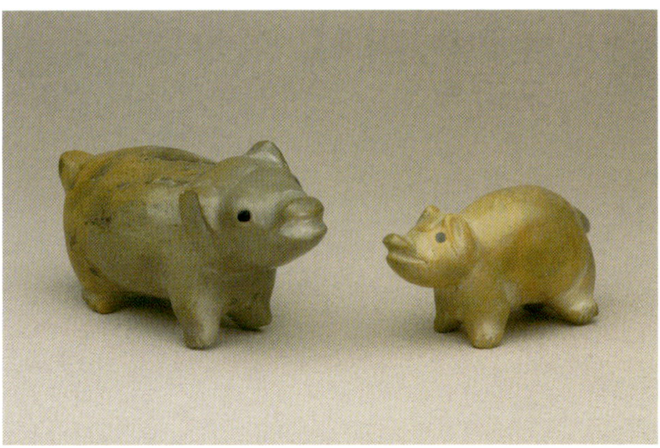

1. Serpentine bear. Length $3\frac{1}{4}$ inches. Collection of Grey Dog Trading Company.

2. Zuni rock bear. Length $4\frac{1}{2}$ inches. Collection of Challis L. Thiessen.

3. Left: Zuni rock bear. Length $3\frac{7}{8}$ inches. Right: Zuni rock bear. Length $2\frac{3}{4}$ inches. Collection of Roger and Mary Crabtree.

4. Zuni rock fox. Length $2\frac{1}{4}$ inches. Collection of Roger and Mary Crabtree.

5. Alabaster bird with silver signature tag. Length $3\frac{1}{8}$ inches. Collection of Roger and Mary Crabtree.

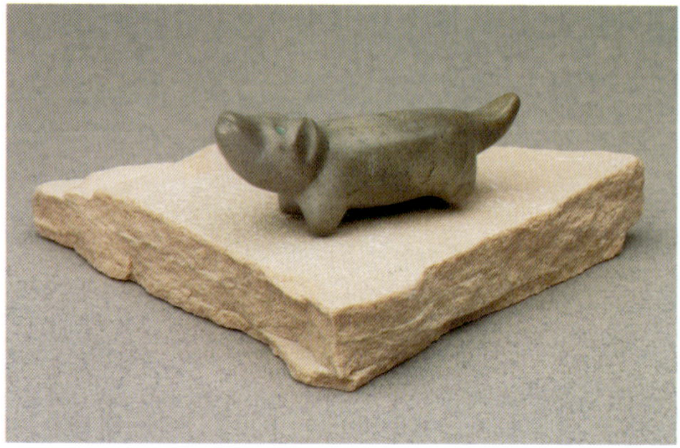

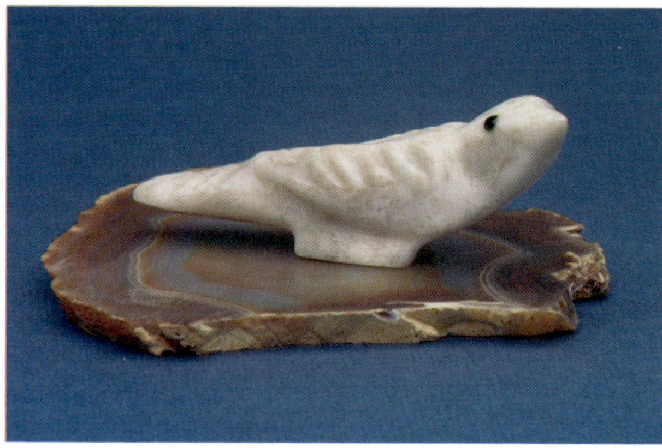

Sadie Laahty

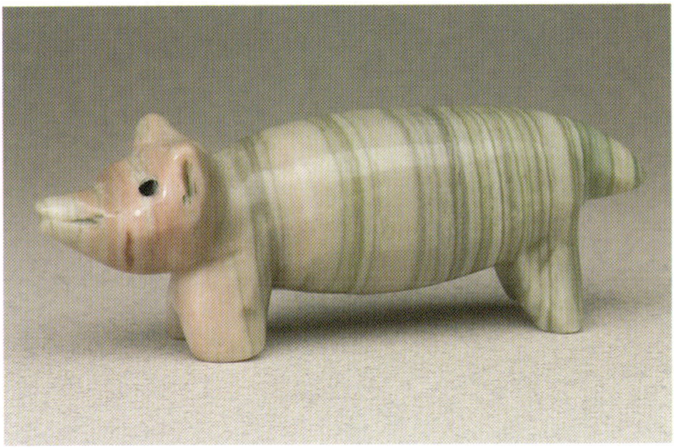

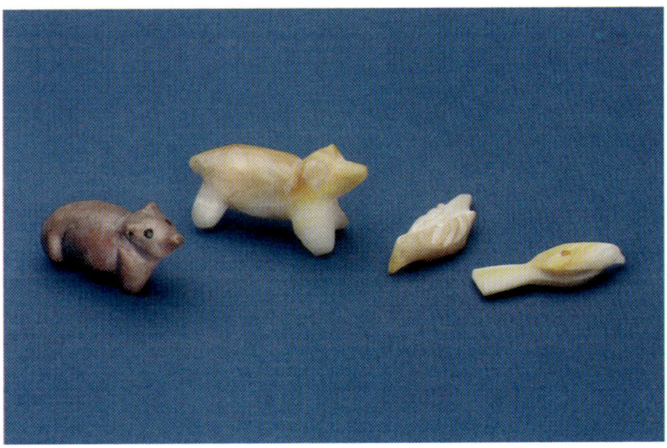

1. Serpentine wolf or bear. Length 2 3/4 inches. Private collection.

2. Left: travertine bear. Length 1 1/8 inches. Collection of the Laahty family. Center: mother-of-pearl wolf or bear (unfinished). Length 1 3/8 inches. Collection of the Laahty family. Right: two mother-of-pearl birds (drilled and unfinished). Length 1 1/8 inches. Private collection.

Alonzo Hustito

1. Serpentine frog. Length 2¾ inches. Collection of Grey Dog Trading Company.

2. Serpentine owl. Height 3⅝ inches. Private collection.

3. Sterling silver squash blossom necklace set with twenty-one turquoise turtles and one turquoise frog; bracelet and ring set with turquoise turtles. Width of naja 3½ inches. Collection of Turkey Mountain Traders.

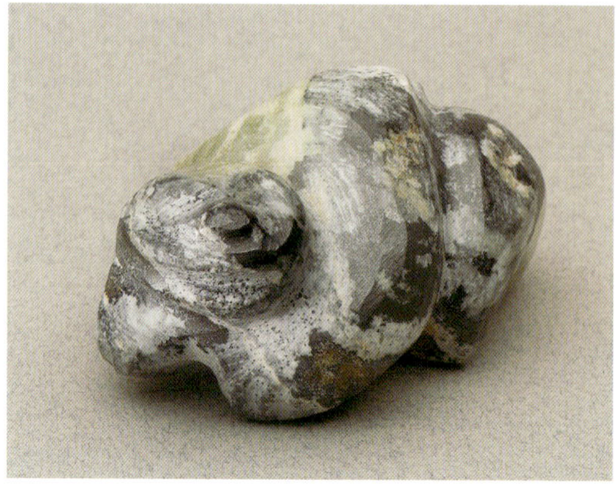

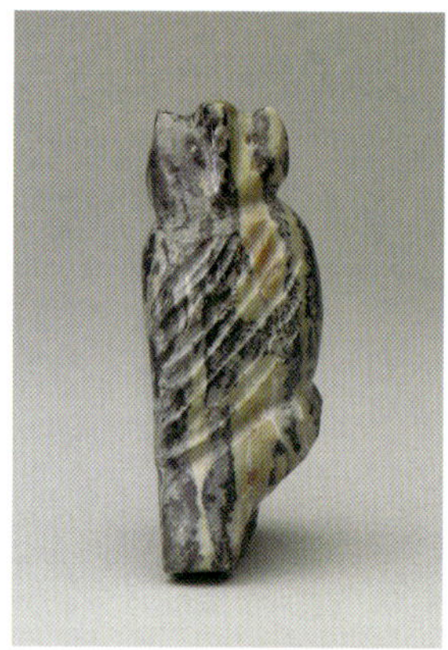

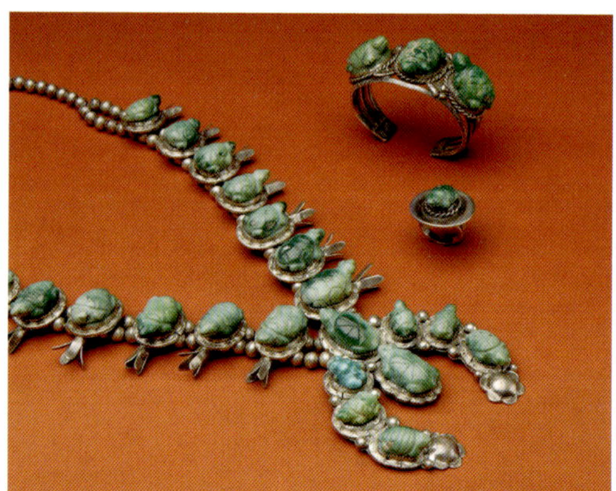

Charles Hustito

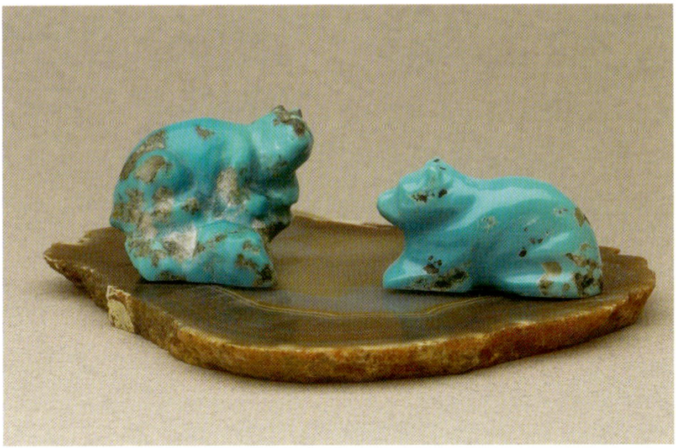

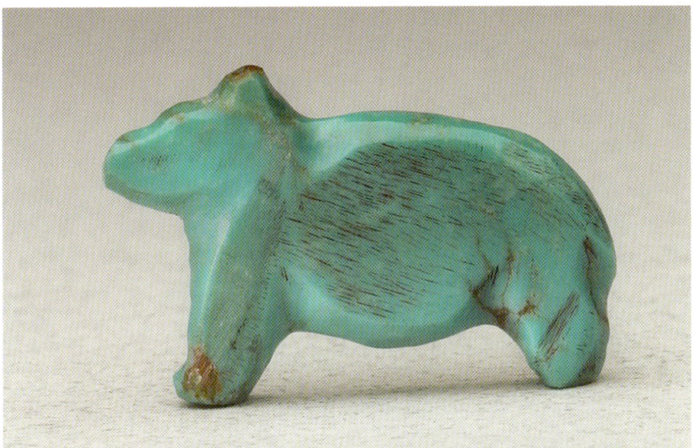

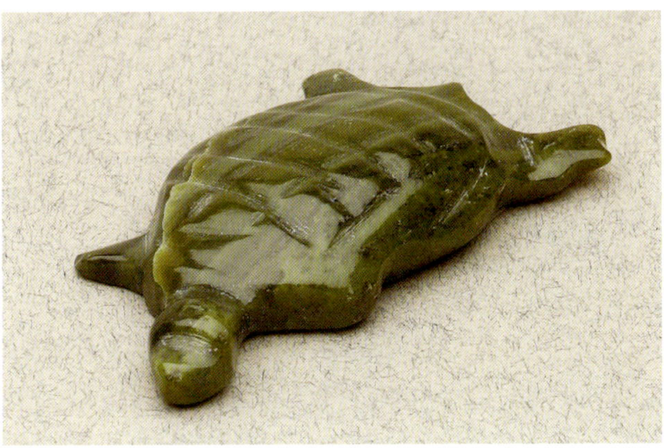

1. Left: turquoise bear. Length 1 1/4 inches. Private collection. Right: turquoise bear. Length 1 3/8 inches. Collection of Grey Dog Trading Company.

2. Turquoise bear. Length 1 inch. Private collection.

3. Serpentine turtle. Length 1 3/4 inches. Private collection.

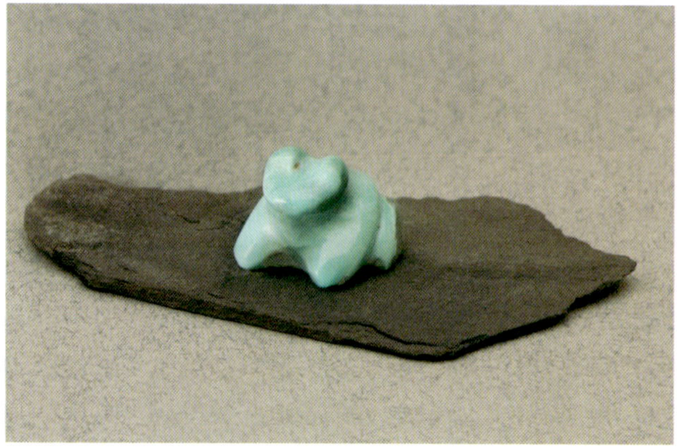

4. Turquoise frog. Length ⅝ inch. Private collection.

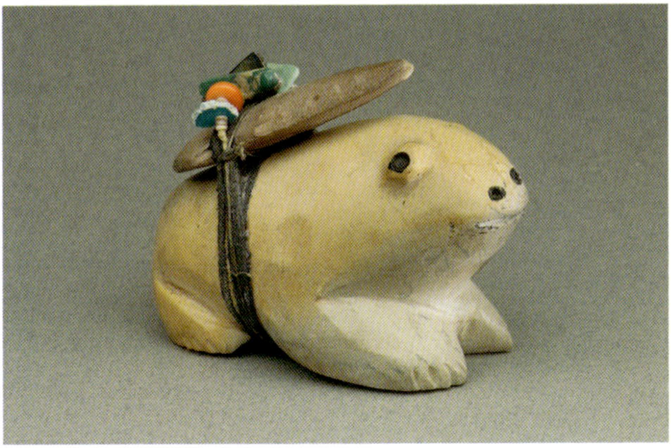

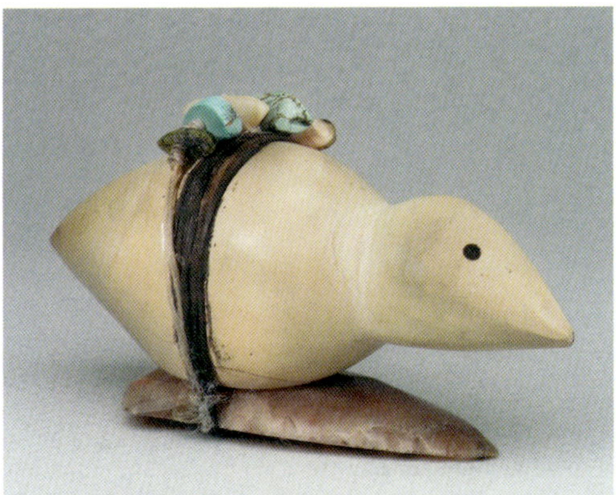

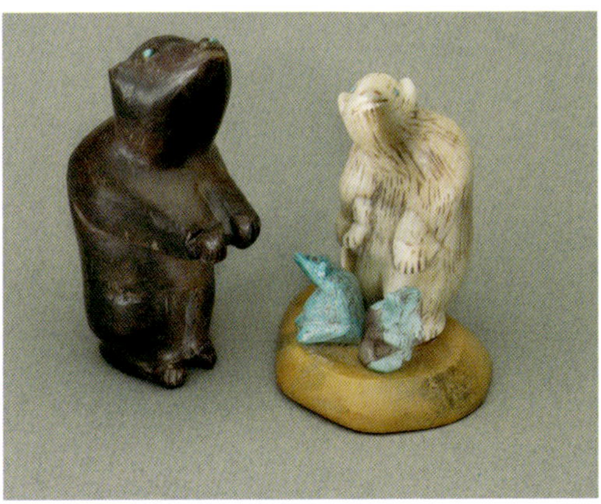

1. Zuni rock frog. Length 3$\frac{5}{8}$ inches. Private collection.

2. Zuni rock eagle. Length 4$\frac{3}{4}$ inches. Collection of Bill Lessard.

3. Left: Nutria travertine standing bear. Height 4$\frac{3}{8}$ inches. Right: travertine and turquoise standing bears on a Zuni rock base. Height 4$\frac{1}{8}$ inches. Collection of Joe and Cindy Tanner, Tanner's Indian Arts, Gallup, New Mexico.

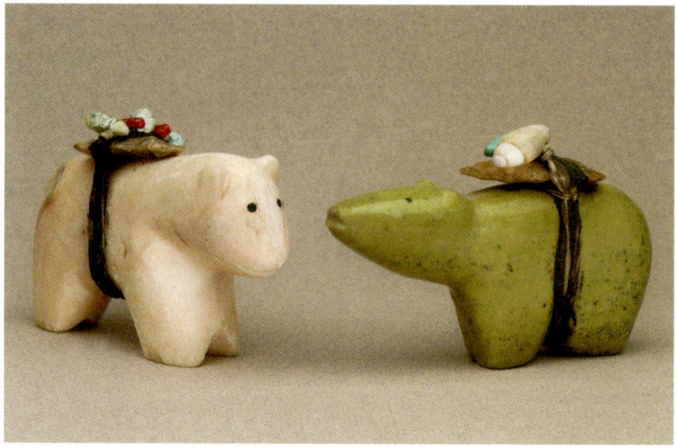

4. Left: alabaster bear. Length 3½ inches. Collection of Jane and Wayne Patterson. Right: serpentine bear. Length 3¾ inches. Collection of Greg Hofmann, Turquoise Village.

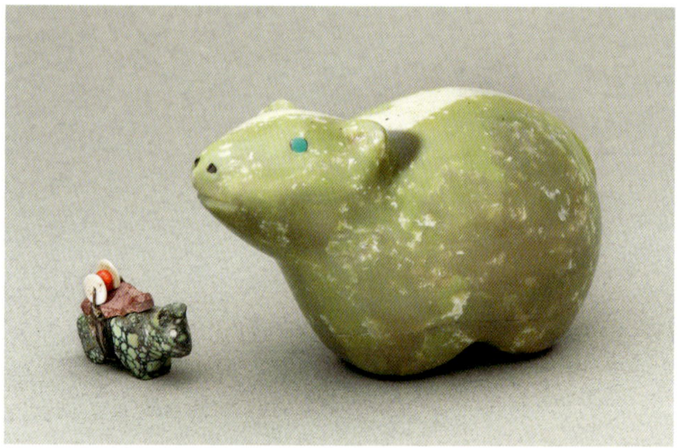

5. Left: variscite bear. Length 1⅛ inches. Collection of Christopher Rex. Right: serpentine bear. Length 3⅞ inches. Collection of Bob Baughman.

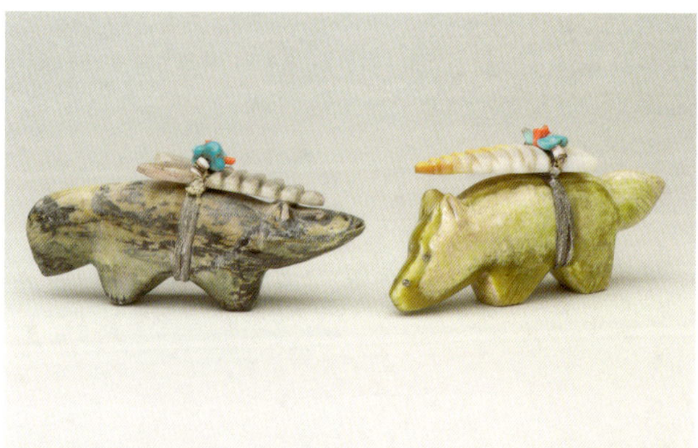

6. Left: serpentine wolf. Length 3⅞ inches. Right: serpentine wolf. Length 4 inches. Collection of Bob Baughman.

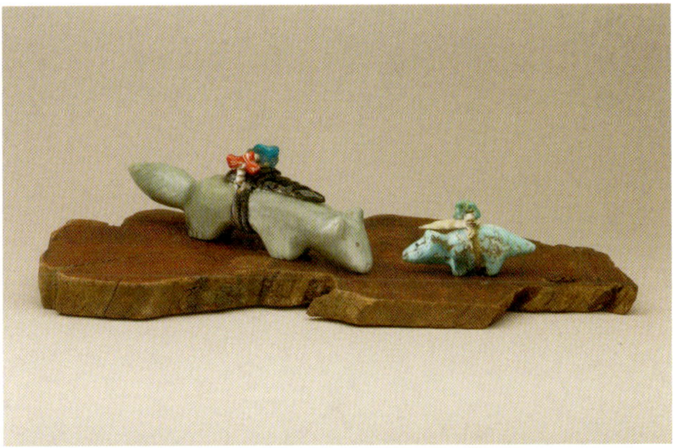

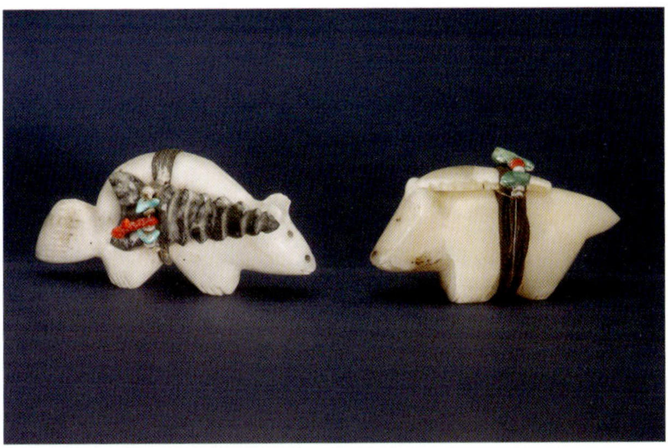

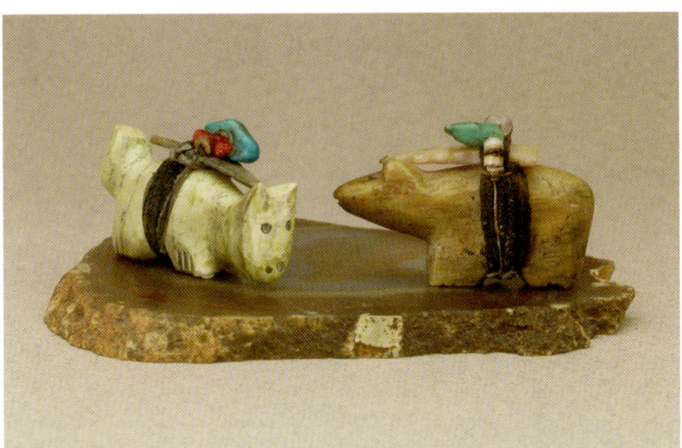

7. Left: serpentine wolf. Length 3¼ inches. Collection of Christopher Rex. Right: turquoise wolf. Length: 1½ inches. Collection of Roger and Mary Crabtree.

8. Left: alabaster wolf. Length 3⅞ inches. Right: onyx wolf or coyote. Length 3¼ inches. Collection of Bob Baughman.

9. Left: serpentine fox. Length 1¾ inches. Private collection. Right: Zuni rock bear. Length 1¾ inches. Collection of Roger and Mary Crabtree.

10. Left: ricolite serpentine mountain lion. Length 2⅛ inches. Collection of Challis L. Thiessen. Right: serpentine eagle. Length 4 inches. Collection of Bob Baughman.

11. Left: serpentine with augite beaver. Length 3 inches. Right: serpentine frog. Length 1⅝ inches. Private collection.

12. Jet wolf with inlaid turquoise stripe. Length 4⅞ inches. Collection of Challis L. Thiessen.

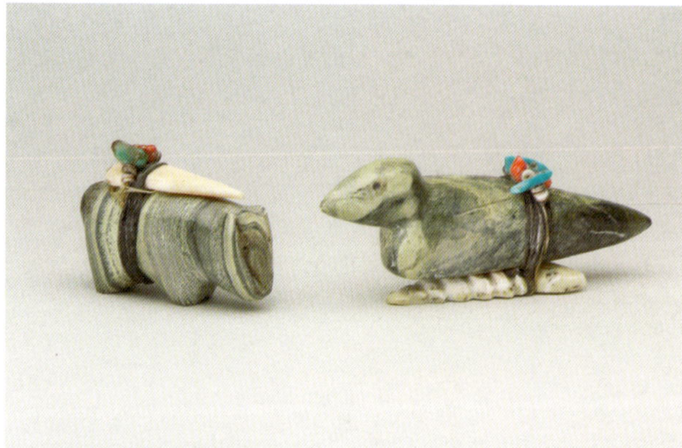

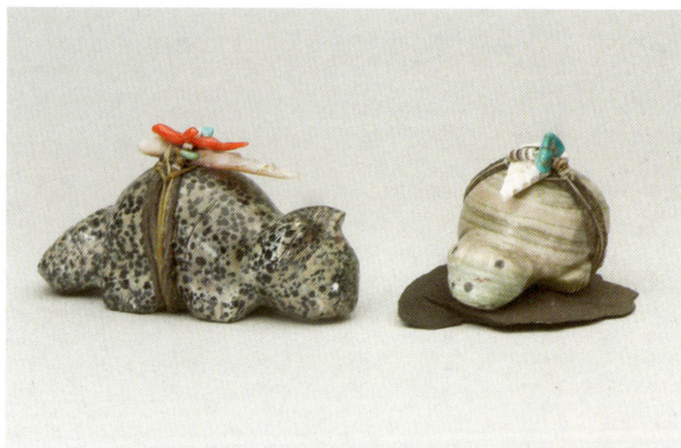

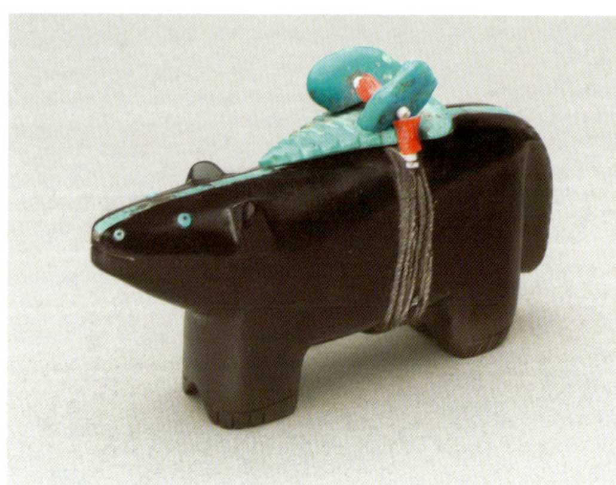

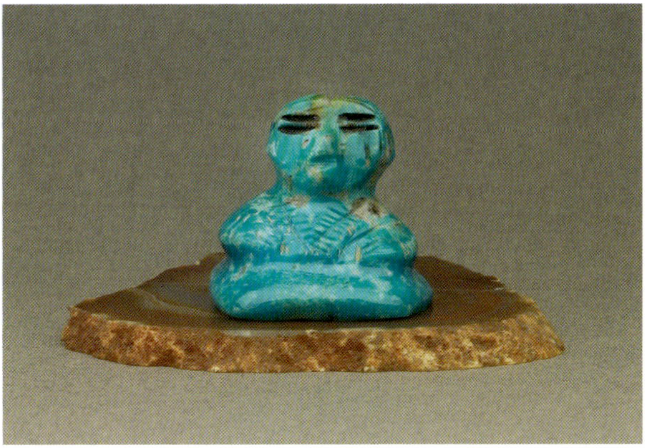

13.Turquoise "altar doll." Height 1½ inches. Private collection.

14. Two-strand fetish necklace with wolves of serpentine, mother-of-pearl, pipestone, turquoise, and jet, strung on olive shell heishi. Longest strand 29½ inches. Collection of Challis L. Thiessen.

15. Detail of fetish necklace. Collection of Challis L. Thiessen.

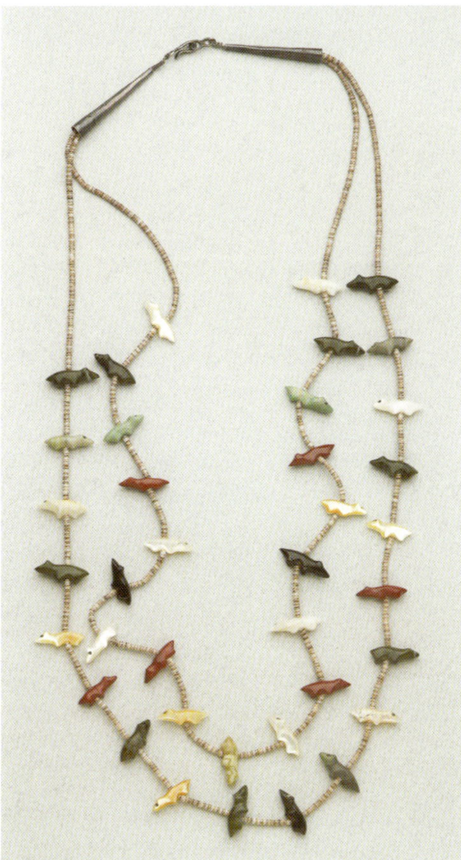

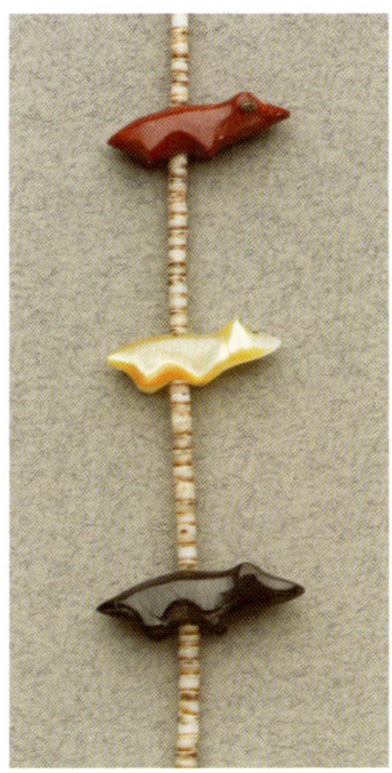

Peter and Dinah Gasper

1. Jet buffalo. Length 6⅝ inches. Collection of Christopher Rex.

2. Jet bear. Length 4⅝ inches. Private collection.

3. Left: jet bear with split inlaid turquoise heartline and inlaid turquoise, gold-lipped mother-of-pearl, and coral stripe. Length 4½ inches. Right: jet bear with split inlaid coral heartline and inlaid coral, turquoise, and gold-lipped mother-of-pearl stripe. Length 3¾ inches. Collection of Challis L. Thiessen.

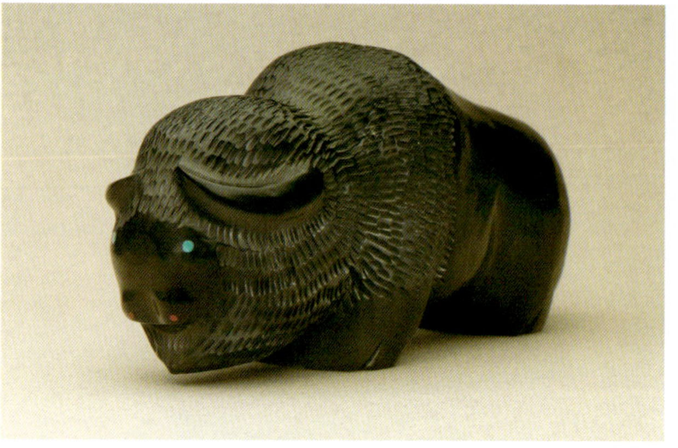

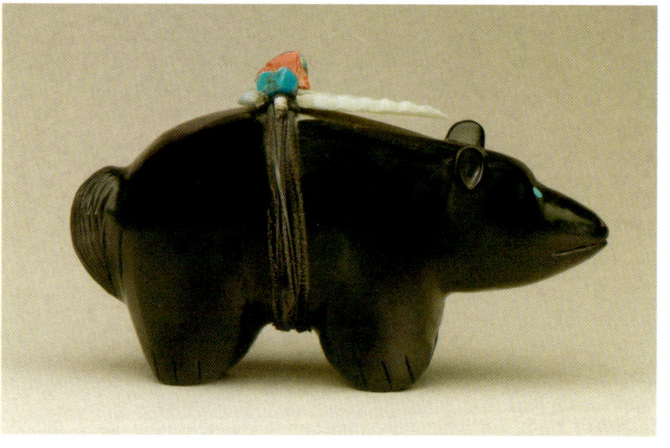

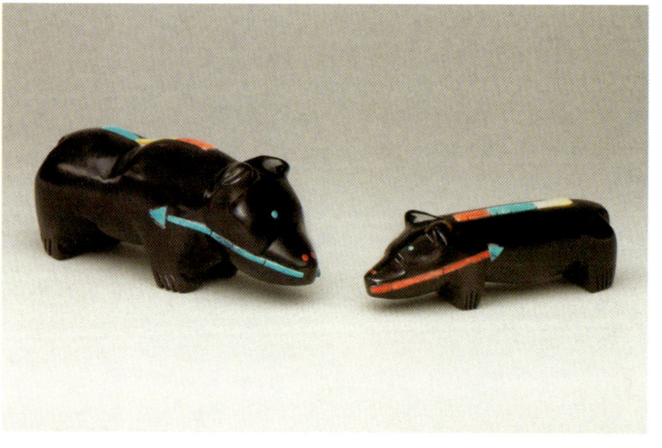

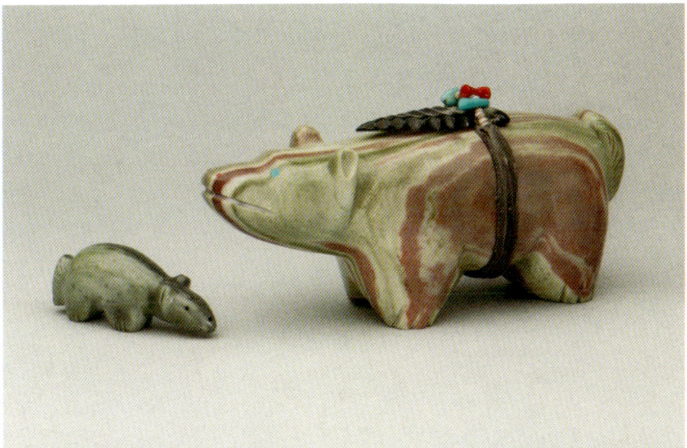

4. Left: serpentine bear. Length 2½ inches. Wheelwright Museum of the American Indian purchase in memory of Challis L. Thiessen. Right: serpentine bear. Length 5¾ inches. Collection of Roger and Mary Crabtree.

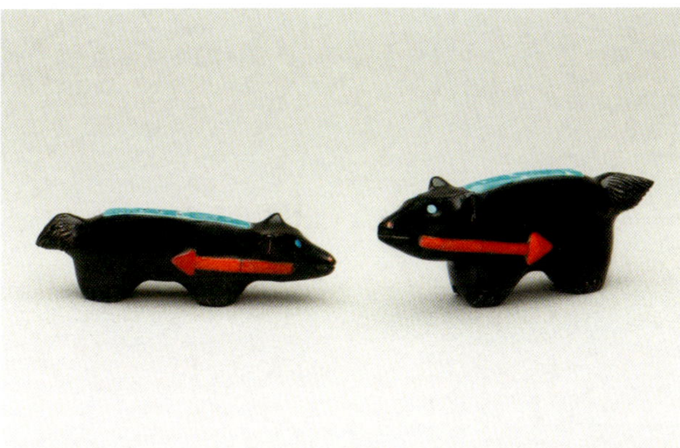

5. Left: jet wolf with split inlaid coral heartline and inlaid turquoise stripe. Length 3¼ inches. Right: jet fox with split inlaid coral heartline and inlaid turquoise stripe. Length 3½ inches. Collection of Challis L. Thiessen.

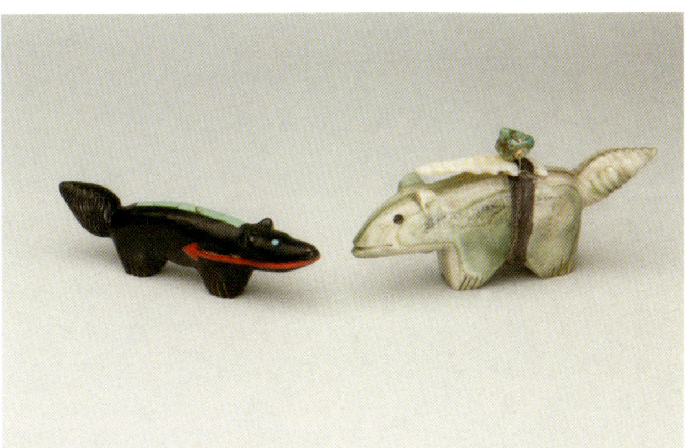

6. Left: jet fox with inlaid coral heartline and inlaid turquoise stripe. Length 3⅛ inches. Private collection. Right: serpentine fox. Length 3⅛ inches. Collection of Christopher Rex.

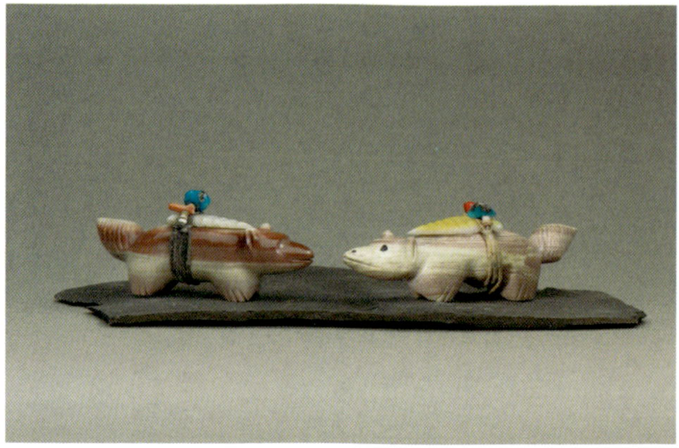

7. Left: serpentine fox. Length 2⅞ inches. Wheelwright Museum of the American Indian purchase in memory of Challis L. Thiessen. Right: serpentine fox. Length 3½ inches. Private collection.

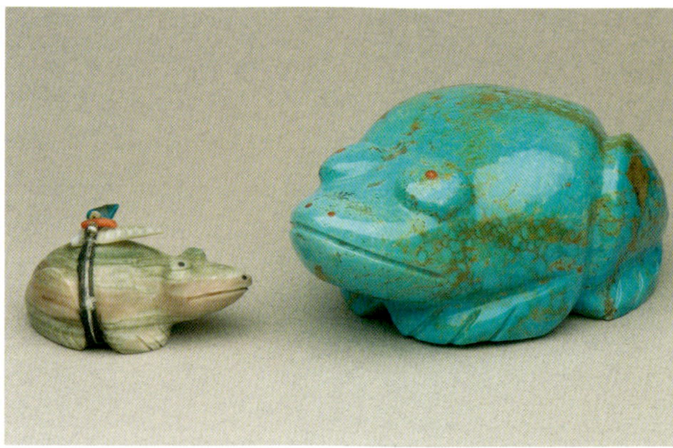

8. Left: serpentine frog. Length 2½ inches. Private collection. Right: turquoise frog. Length 5 inches. Collection of Greg Hofmann, Turquoise Village.

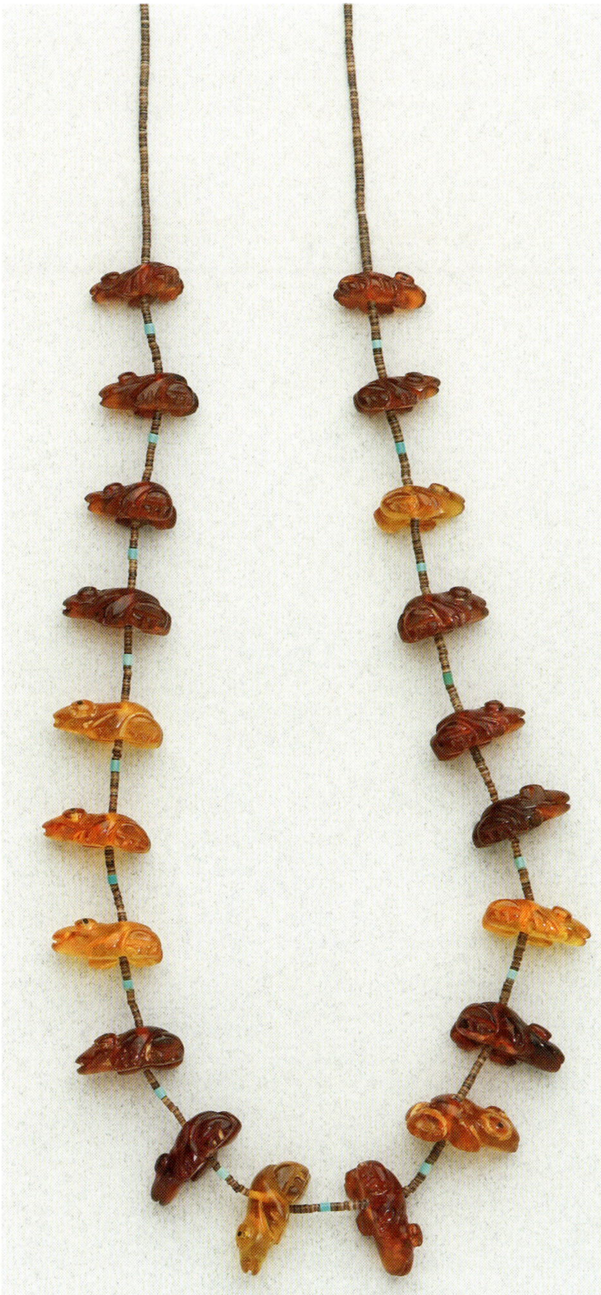

9. Fetish necklace with amber frogs, strung on olive shell heishi. Length 25 inches. Private collection.

Rignie and Lena Boone

1. Left: alabaster fox by Lena Boone. Length 4¼ inches. Private collection. Right: Picasso marble fox by Lena Boone. Length 3 inches. Collection of Andrews Pueblo Pottery.

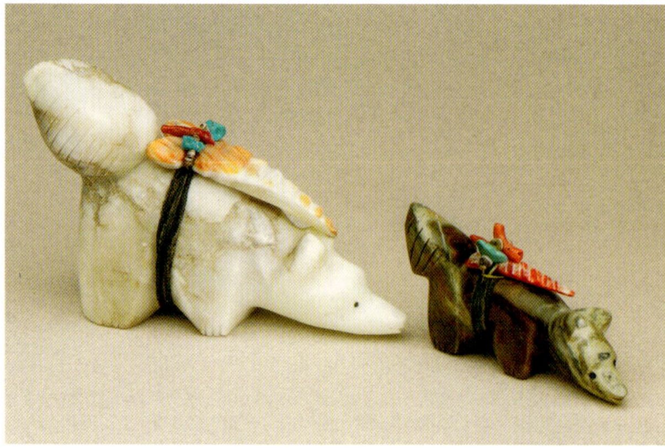

2. Left: travertine onyx bear by Rignie and Lena Boone. Length 3⅞ inches. Right: serpentine frog by Lena Boone. Length 3⅞ inches. Private collection.

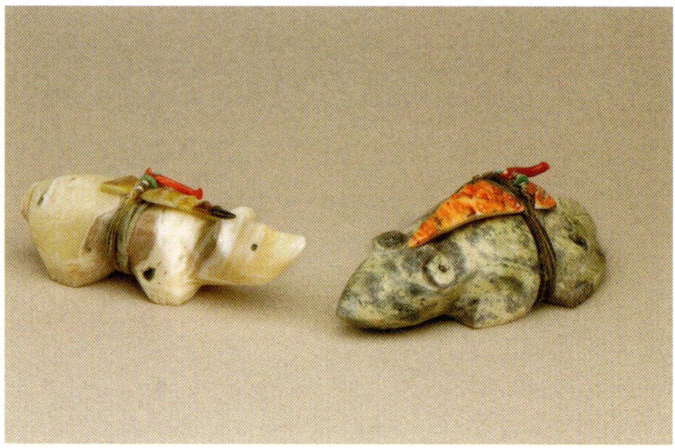

3. Left: turquoise wolf or fox by Rignie and Lena Boone. Length 1⅜ inches. Collection of Grey Dog Trading Company. Right: serpentine fox by Rignie and Lena Boone. Length 3 inches. Private collection.

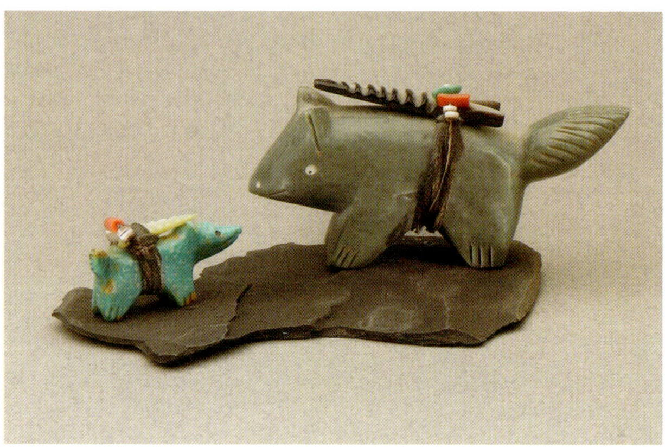

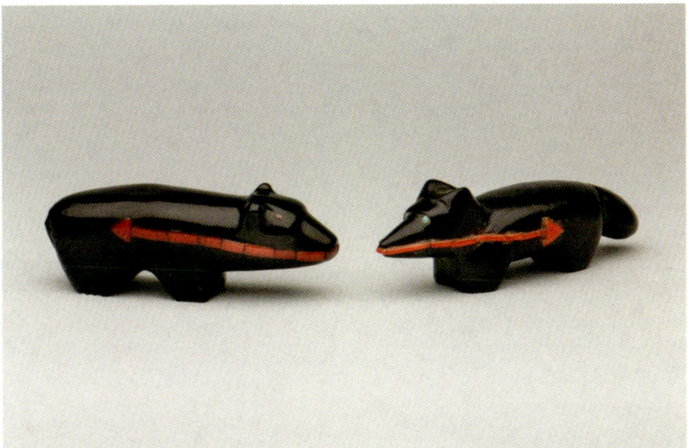

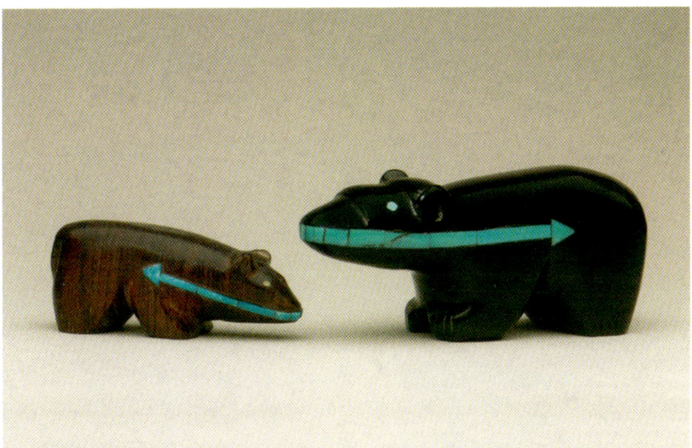

4. Left: jet bear with inlaid coral heartline by Rignie Boone. Length 2⅞ inches. Collection of Roger and Mary Crabtree. Right: jet wolf with inlaid coral heartline by Rignie Boone. Length 3½ inches. Collection of Grey Dog Trading Company.

5. Left: ironwood bear with inlaid turquoise heartline by Rignie Boone. Length 3½ inches. Right: jet bear with inlaid turquoise heartline by Rignie Boone. Length 4¼ inches. Private collection.

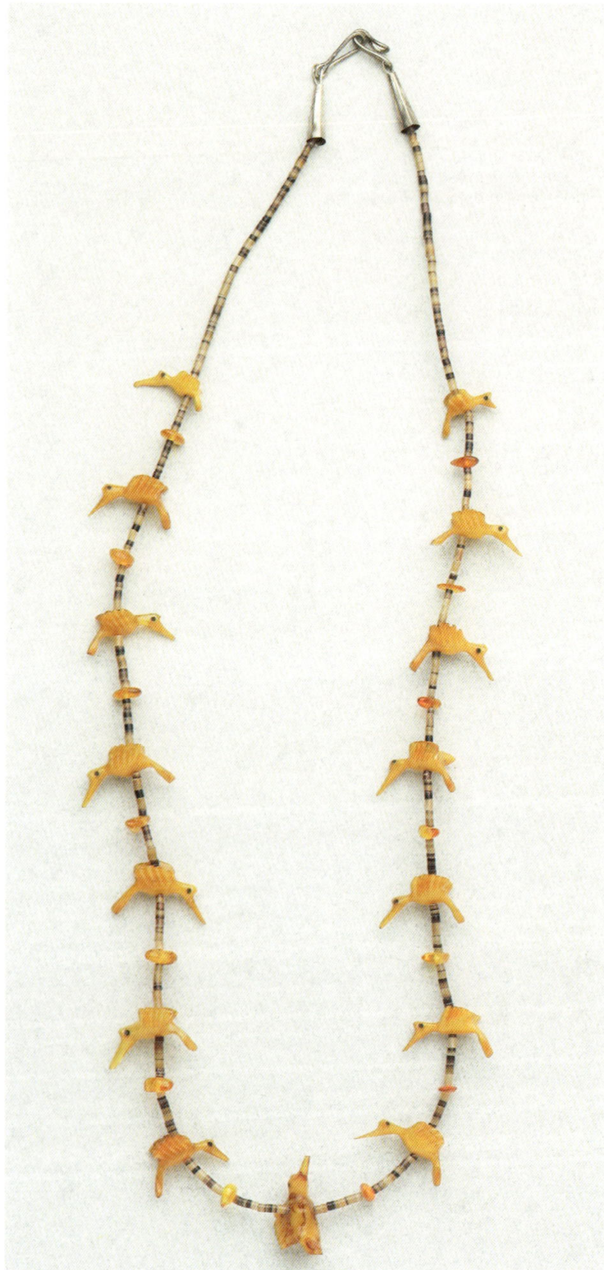

6. Fetish necklace with amber hummingbirds by Rignie Boone. Strung on shell heishi. Length 25 inches. Collection of Challis L. Thiessen.

Bobby Lonasee

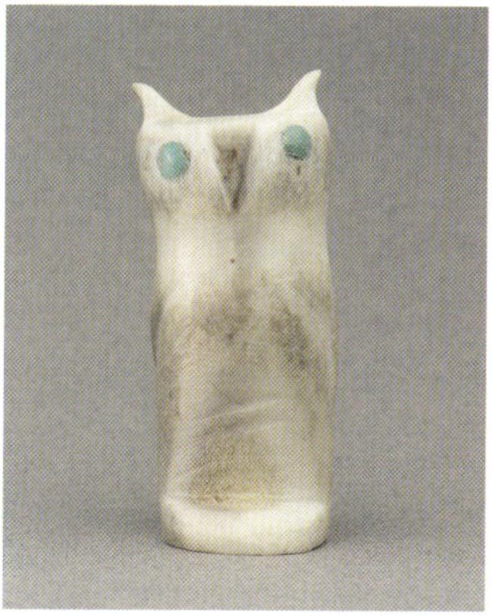

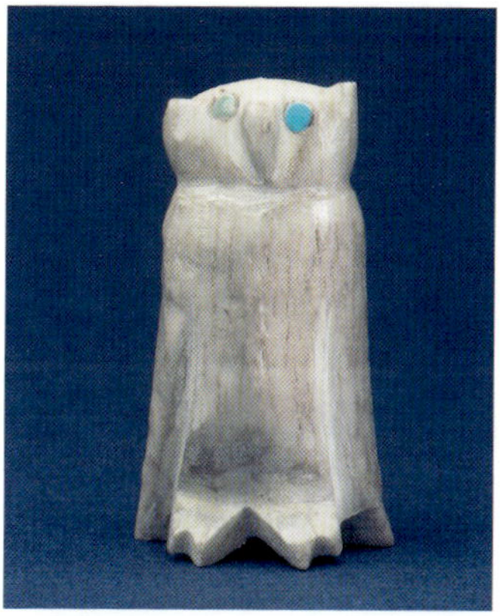

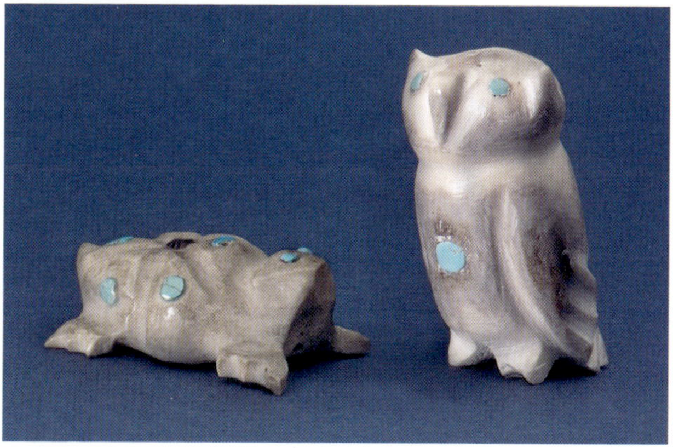

1. Antler owl. Height 2¾ inches. Collection of Grey Dog Trading Company.

2. Antler owl. Height 1⅞ inches. Private collection.

3. Left: antler turtle. Length 1⅝ inches. Right: antler owl. Height 2 inches. Collection of Christopher Rex.

4. Antler turtle. Length 2 inches. Private collection.

5. Antler frog. Length 1 3/8 inches. Collection of Dick Wessman.

6. Left: antler hummingbird. Height 2 3/8 inches.
Right: antler hummingbird. Height 2 5/8 inches. Private collection.

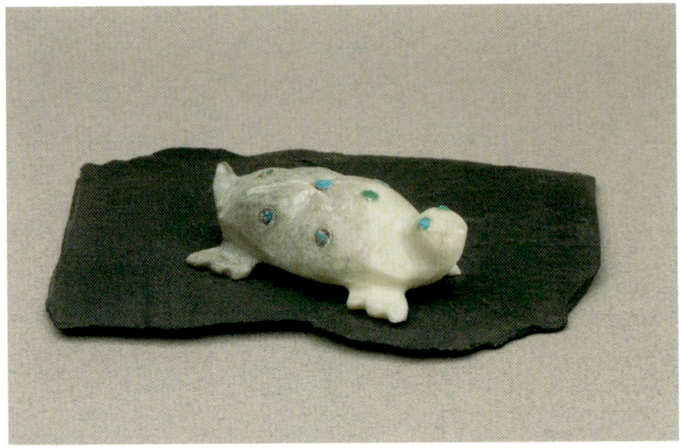

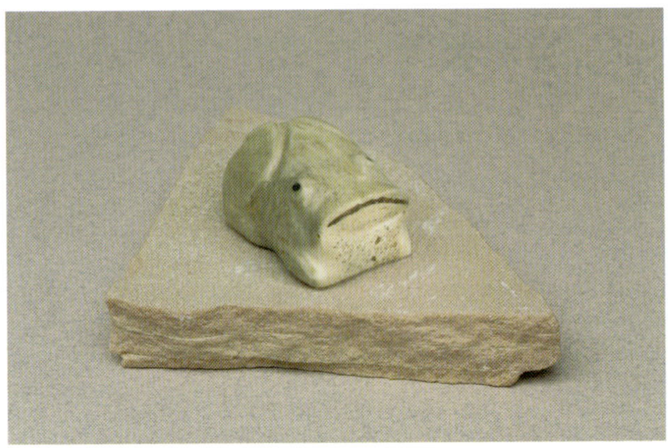

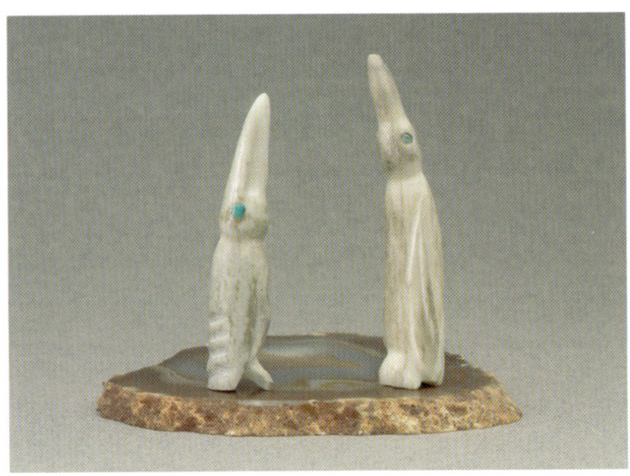

Sepo Ponchuella

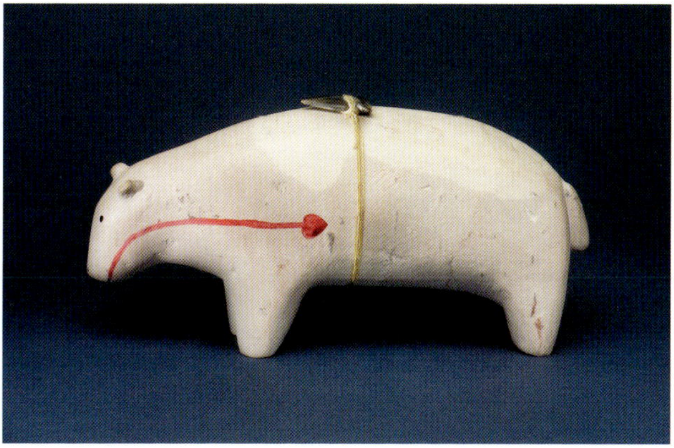

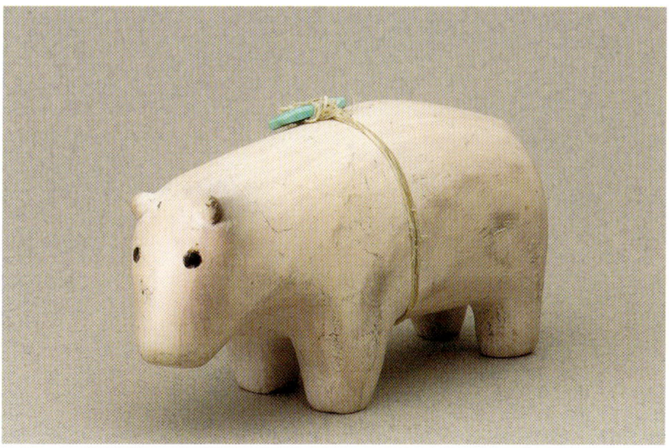

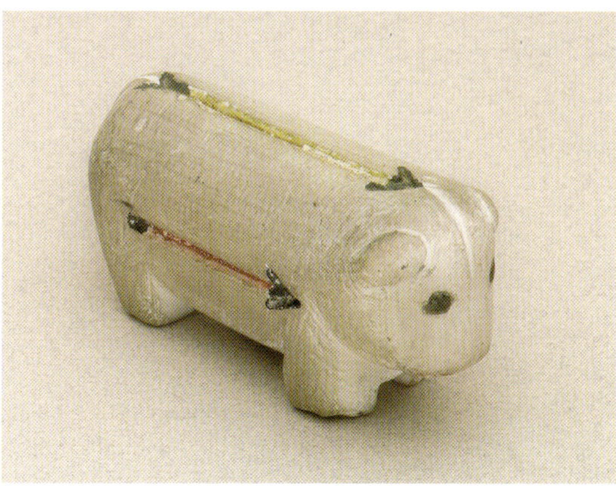

1. Ojo rock bear with painted heartline. Length 8⅜ inches. Collection of Grey Dog Trading Company.

2. Ojo rock bear. Length 4 inches. Private collection.

3. Ojo rock bear with carved and painted arrows. Length 3⅜ inches. Collection of Grey Dog Trading Company.

Rosalia Quam

1. Serpentine frog. Length 3⅝ inches. Collection of Bob Baughman.

2. Clockwise from left: serpentine frog. Length 2⅛ inches. Private collection. Pipestone frog. Height 1⅜ inches. Collection of Greg Hofmann, Turquoise Village. Serpentine frog. Length 2⅛ inches. Collection of Grey Dog Trading Company. Serpentine frog. Length 1¼ inches. Private collection.

3. Left: antler owl. Height 2¼ inches. Center: antler owl. Height 1¼ inches. Right: mother-of-pearl owl. Length 2 inches. Private collections.

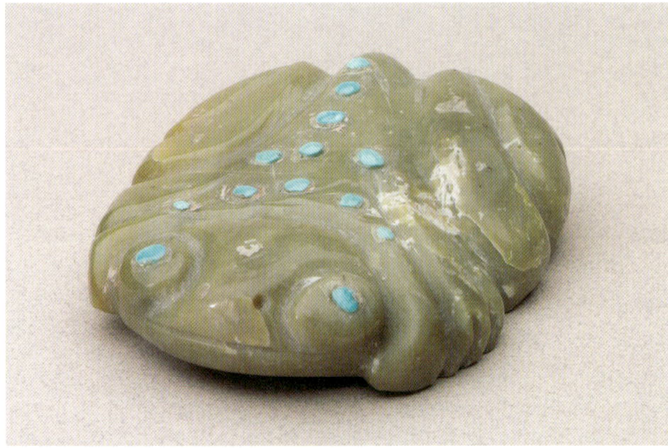

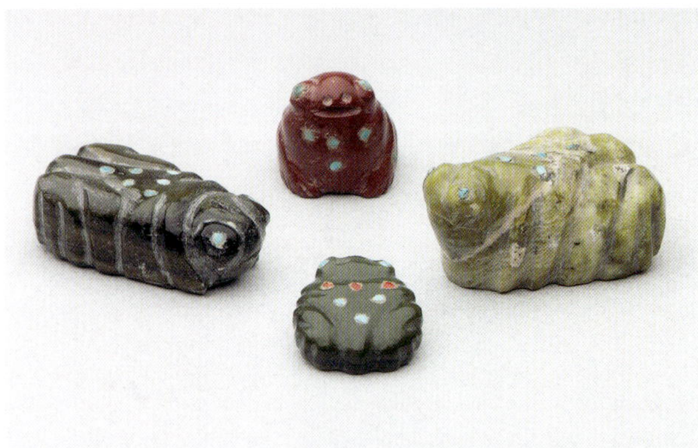

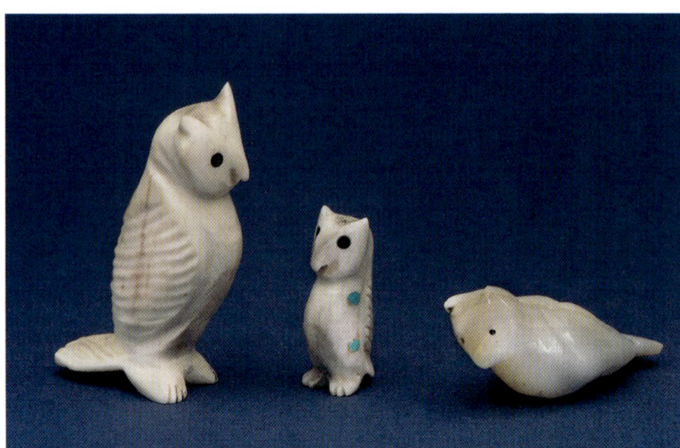

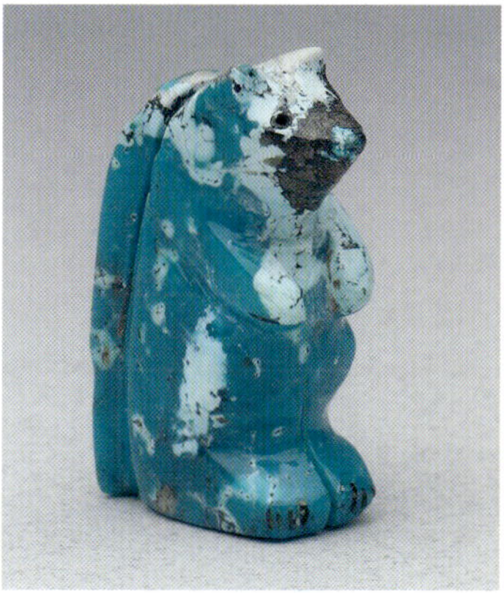

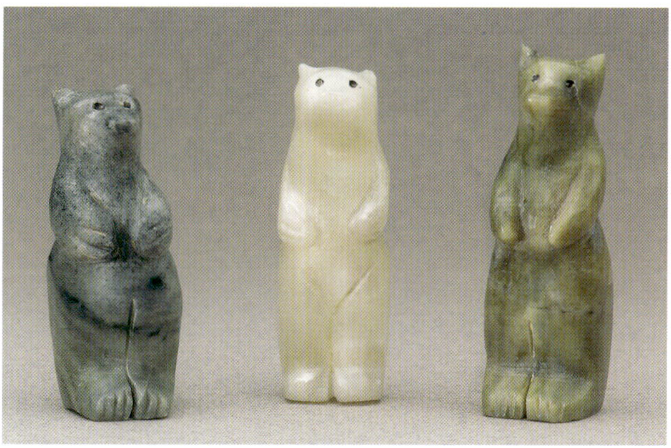

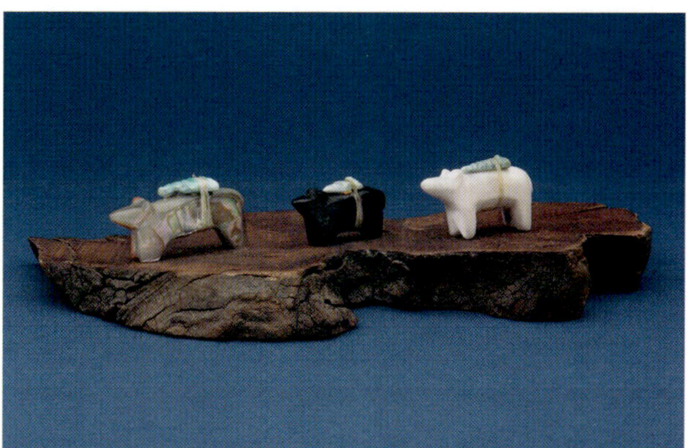

4. Turquoise standing squirrel. Height 1 3/8 inches. Private collection.

5. Left: serpentine standing bear. Height 1 3/4 inches. Center: travertine onyx standing bear. Height 1 7/8 inches. Right: serpentine standing bear. Height 2 inches. Private collections.

6. Left: abalone bear. Length 1 1/2 inches. Collection of Bob Baughman. Center: jet bear. Length 1 1/4 inches. Private collection. Right: alabaster bear. Length 1 1/4 inches. Private collection.

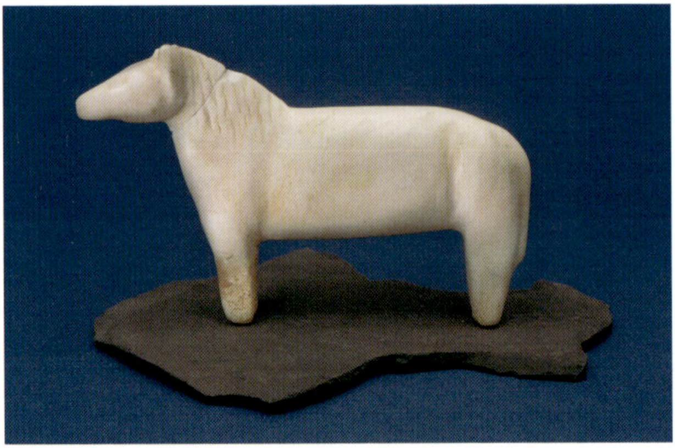

7. Alabaster horse. Length 3⅜ inches. Private collection.

Andrew Emerson Quam

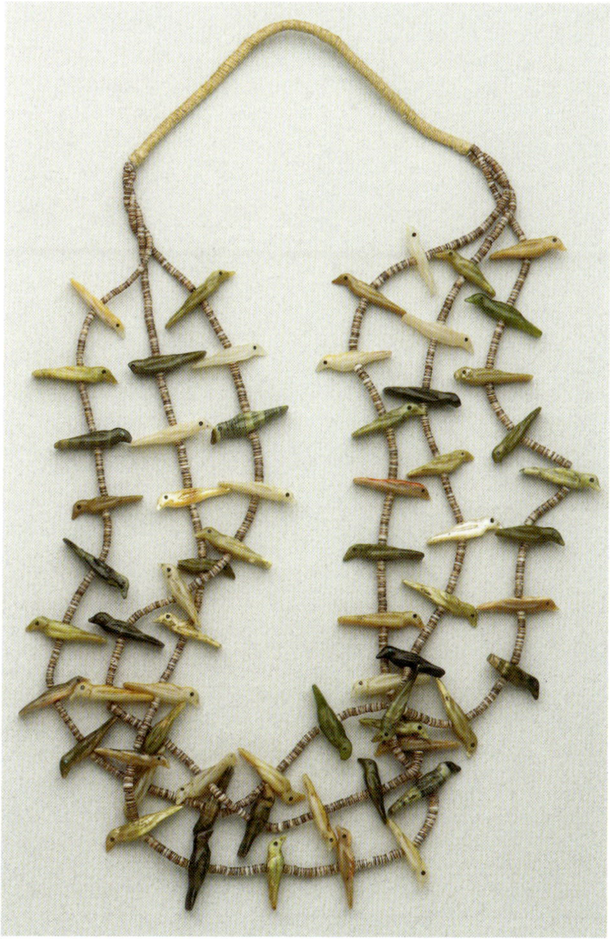

1. Three-strand fetish necklace with birds of serpentine, mother-of-pearl, and abalone, strung on olive shell heishi. Longest strand 31½ inches. Collection of Challis L. Thiessen.

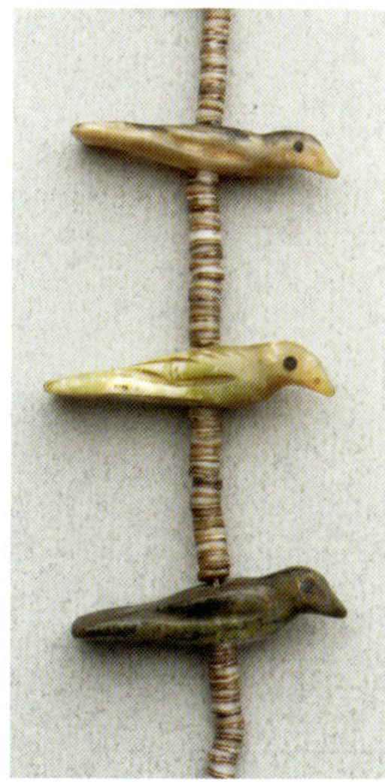

2. Detail of fetish necklace. Collection of Challis L. Thiessen.

George Cheechee Haloo

1. Fetish necklace with birds of mother-of-pearl and abalone, strung on olive shell heishi. Length 27 inches. Private collection.

2. Detail of fetish necklace. Private collection.

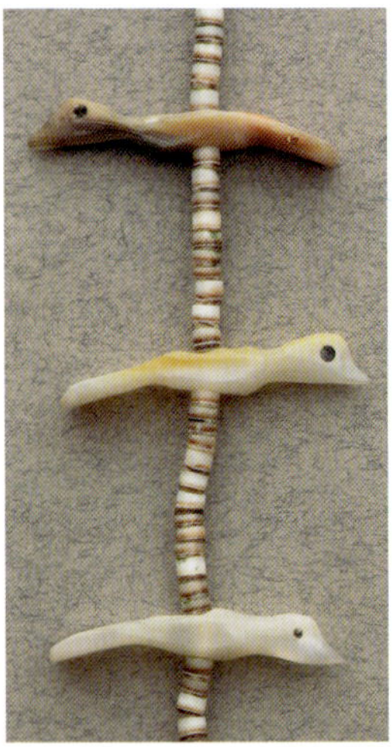

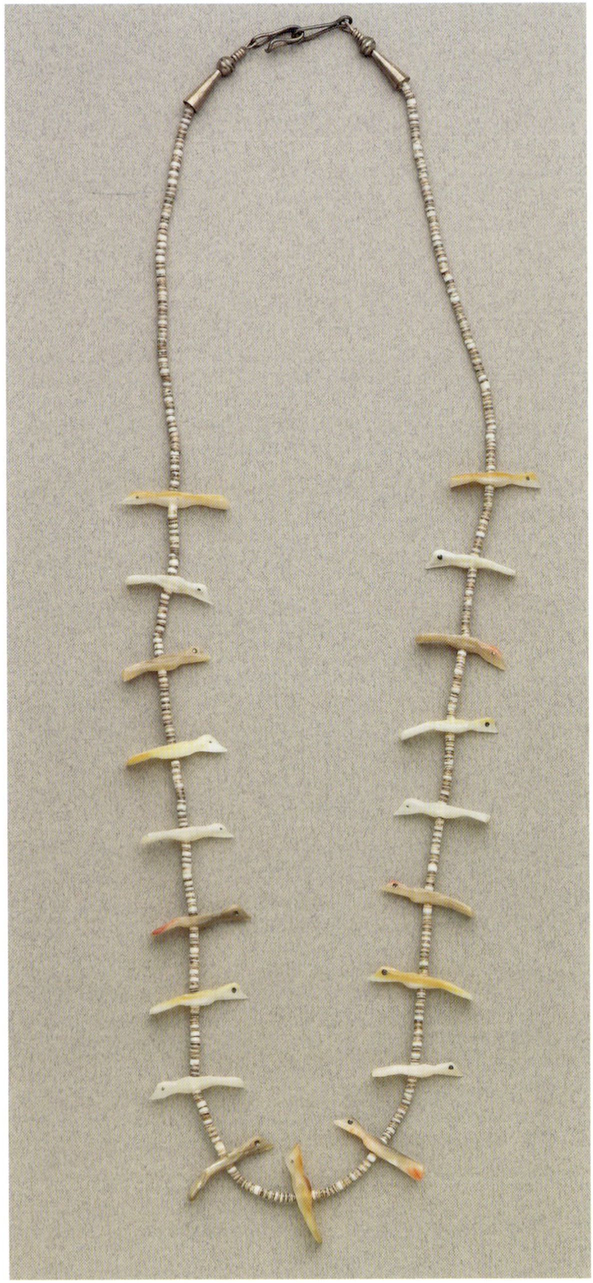

Ellen Quandelacy

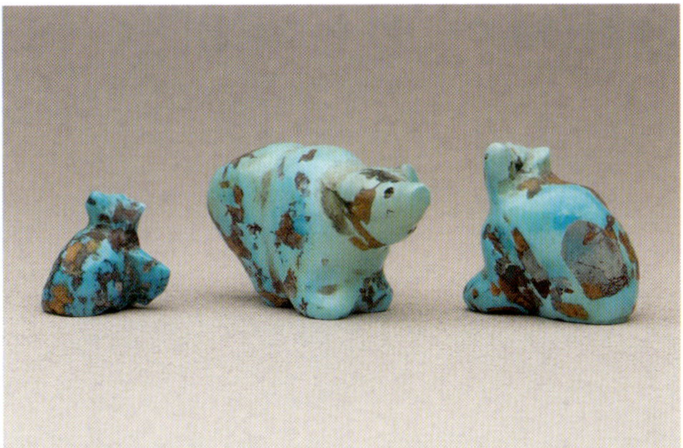

1. Left: natural turquoise bear. Height ¾ inch. Center: natural turquoise bear. Length 1¾ inches. Right: natural turquoise bear. Height 1⅛ inches. Private collection.

Andres Quandelacy

1. Ironwood buffalo with inlaid coral mouth. Length $3\frac{7}{8}$ inches. Private collection.

2. Left: natural turquoise buffalo. Length $2\frac{7}{8}$ inches. Private collection. Right: mother-of-pearl buffalo with inlaid coral mouth. Length $1\frac{7}{8}$ inches. Wheelwright Museum of the American Indian purchase in memory of Challis Thiessen.

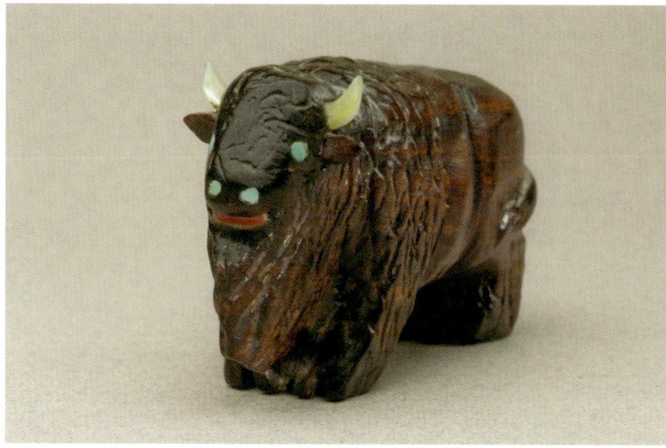

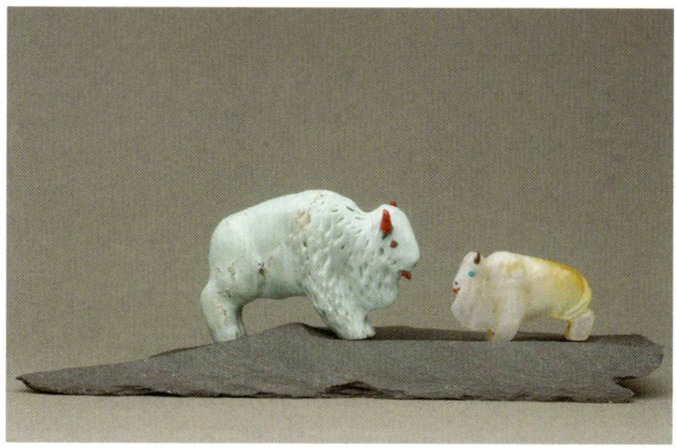

Barlow Quandelacy

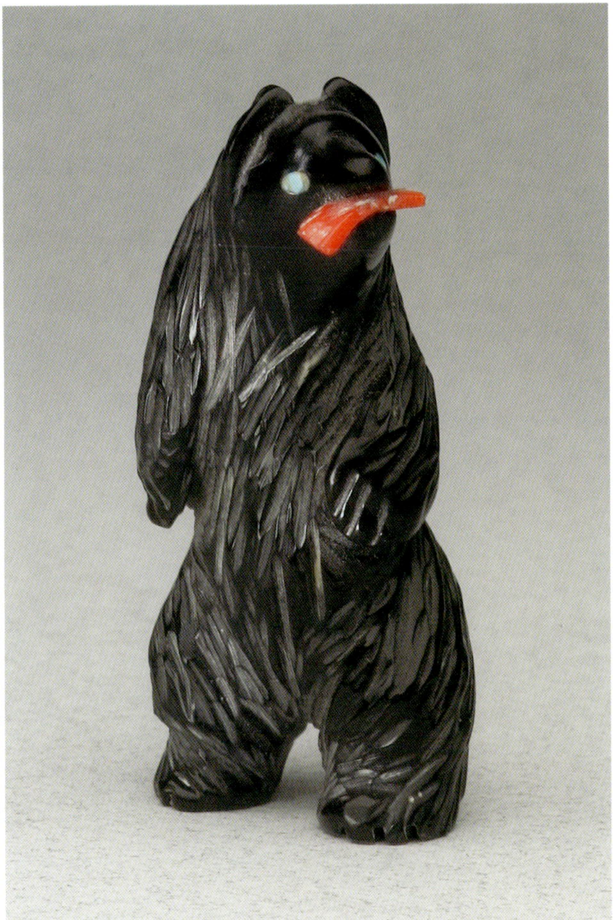

1. Jet standing bear with coral fish. Height 1¾ inches. Collection of Grey Dog Trading Company.

Faye Quandelacy

1. Alabaster maiden with mother-of-pearl, coral, and turquoise corn. Height 4¼ inches. Private collection.

2. Left: turquoise Corn Maiden. Height 1⅜ inches. Right: turquoise turtle. Length 1⅜ inches. Private collection.

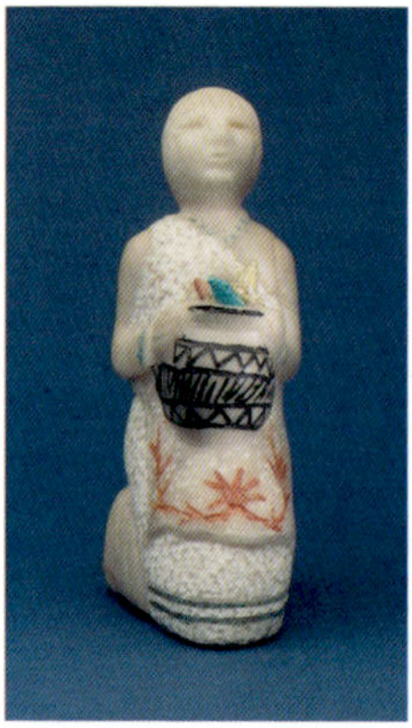

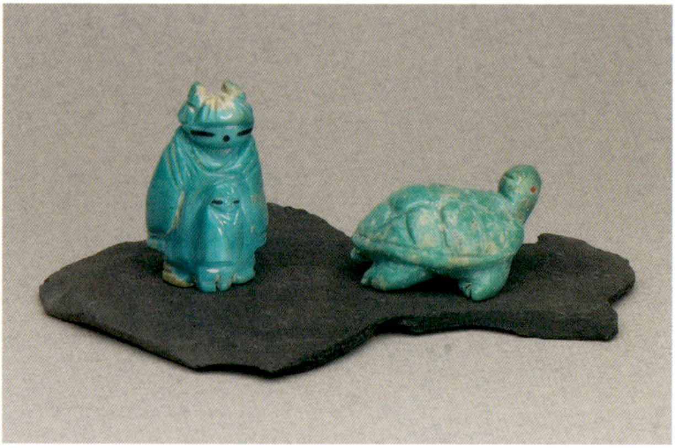

Stewart Quandelacy

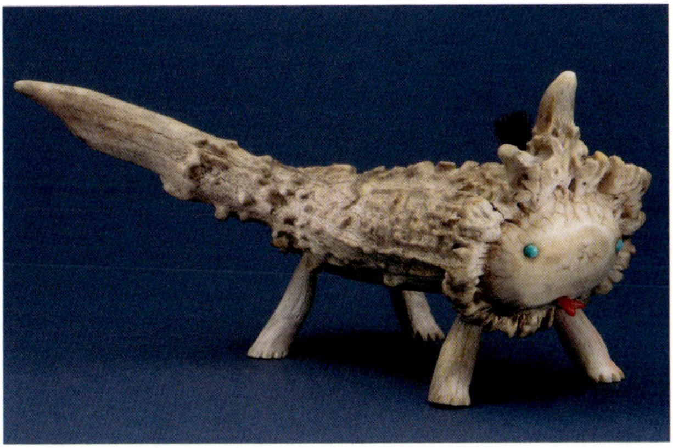

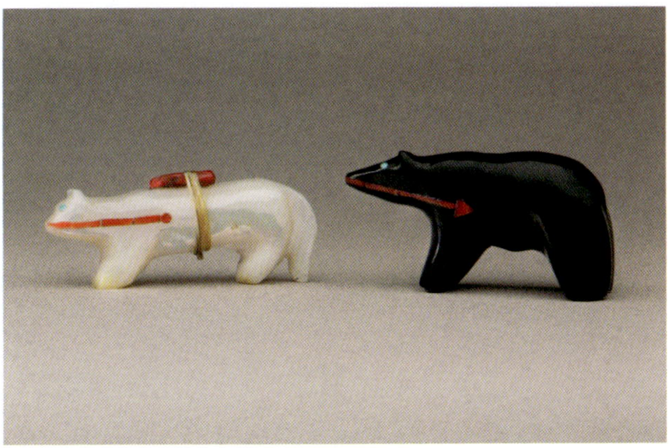

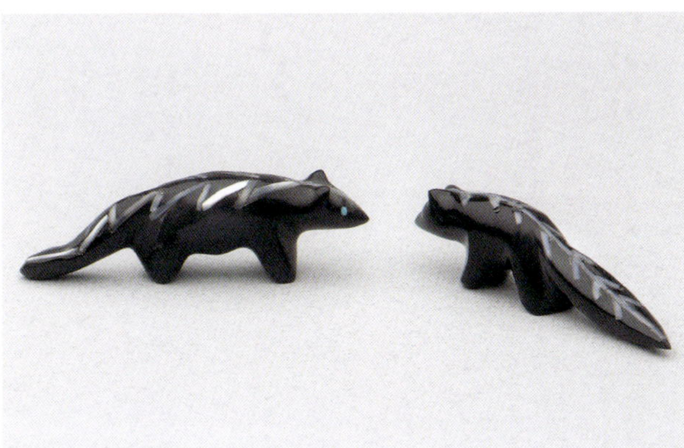

1. Antler "Ugly Monster." Length $5\frac{3}{4}$ inches. Originally made by Stewart or Dickie Quandelacy with insets finished by Stewart in 2004. Collection of Stewart Quandelacy.

2. Left: mother-of-pearl mountain lion with inlaid coral heartline. Length $2\frac{3}{8}$ inches. Right: jet bear with inlaid coral heartline. Length $2\frac{1}{4}$ inches. Wheelwright Museum of the American Indian purchase in memory of Challis L. Thiessen.

3. Left: jet skunk with inlaid mother-of-pearl markings. Length $2\frac{1}{8}$ inches. Private collection. Right: jet skunk with inlaid mother-of-pearl markings. Length $2\frac{1}{8}$ inches. Wheelwright Museum of the American Indian purchase in memory of Challis L. Thiessen.

4. Jet turtle with inlaid turquoise segments. Length 4¼ inches. Private collection.

5. Sandstone buffalo with painted and incised heart-line. Length 10½ inches. Collection of Stewart Quandelacy.

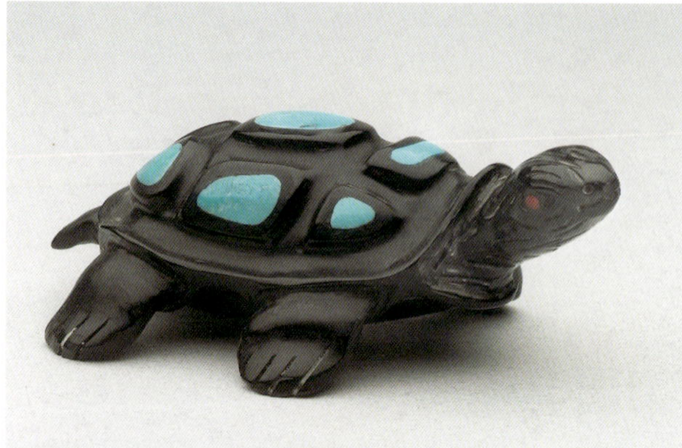

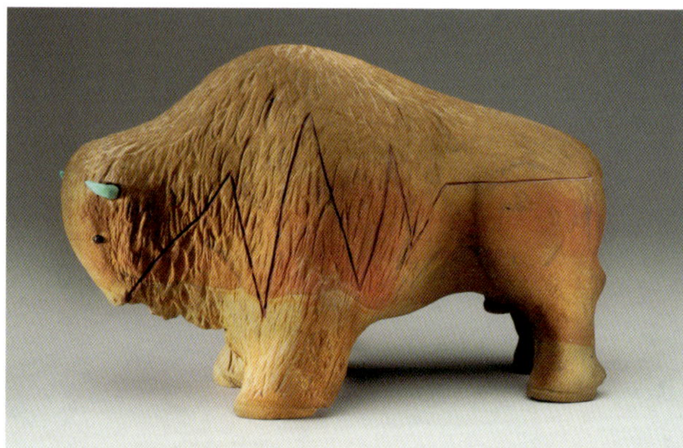

Pernell Gasper

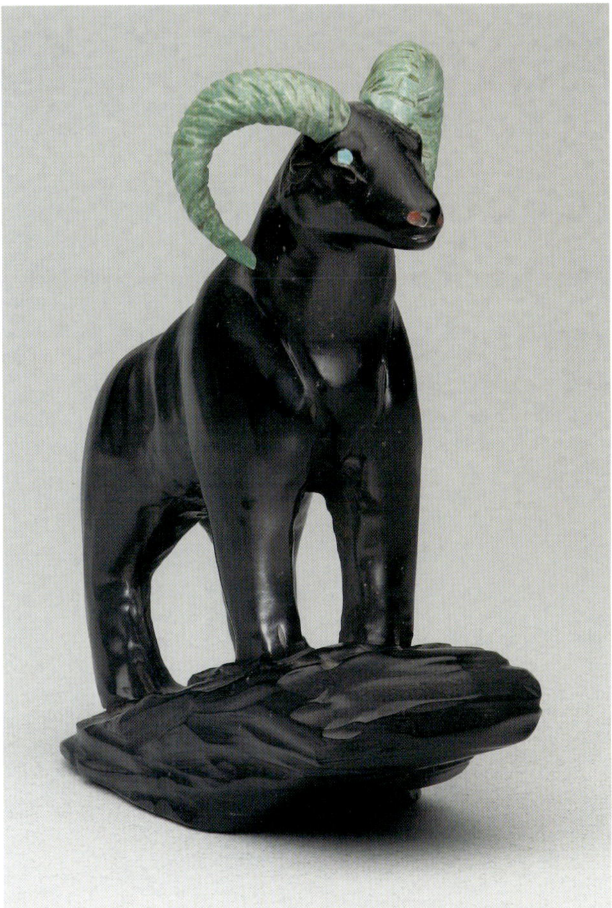

1. Jet ram. Height 4 inches.
Private collection.

Aaron and Thelma Sheche

1. Serpentine man and woman. Height of man 5⅞ inches. Private collection.

2. Serpentine man and woman. Height of man 2¾ inches. Private collection.

3. Nutria travertine sitting bear. Height 1¼ inches. Collection of Roger and Mary Crabtree.

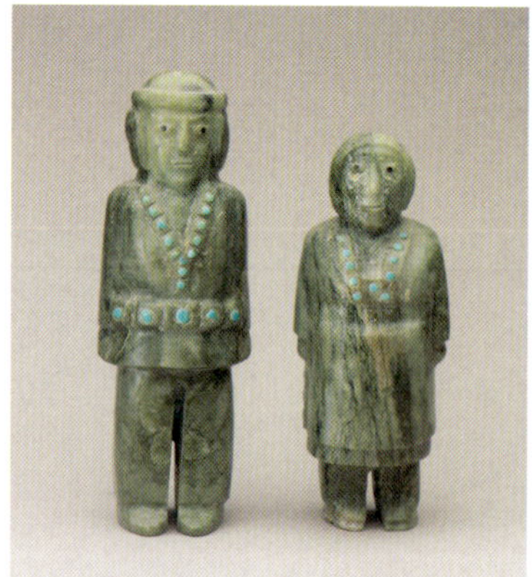

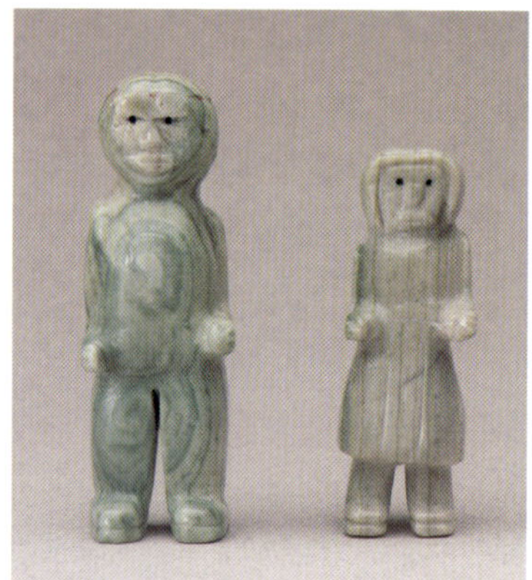

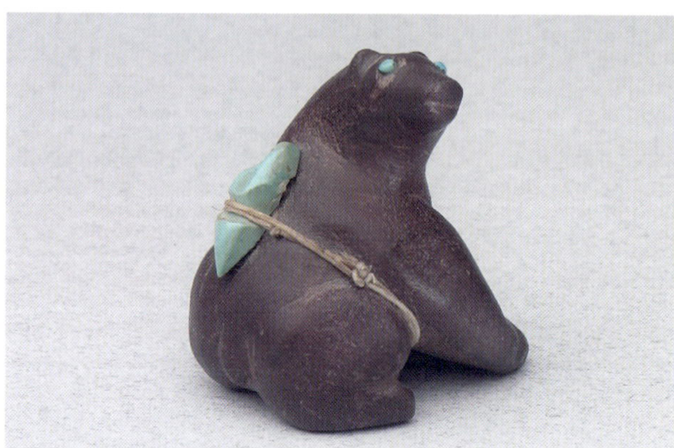

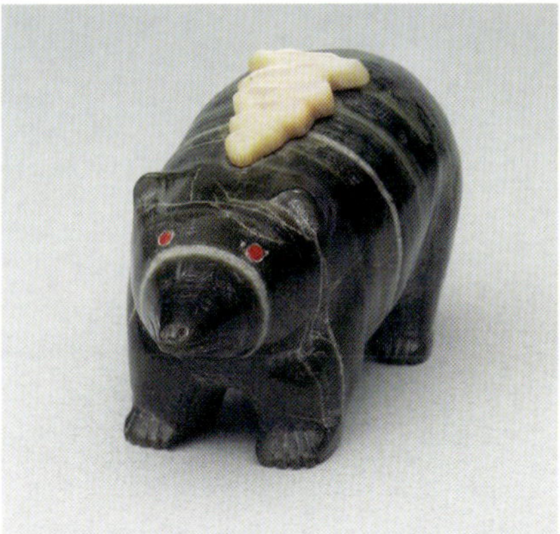

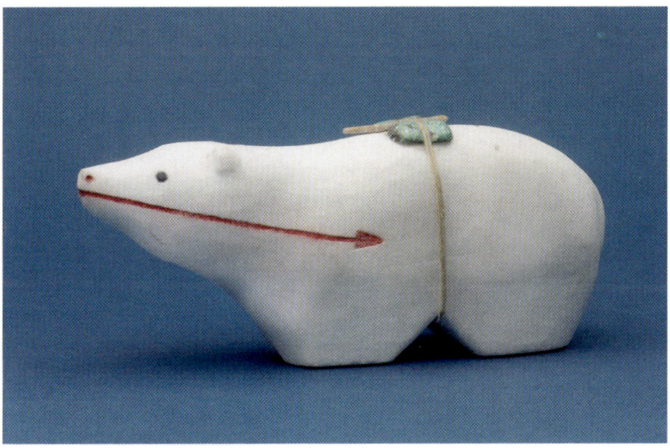

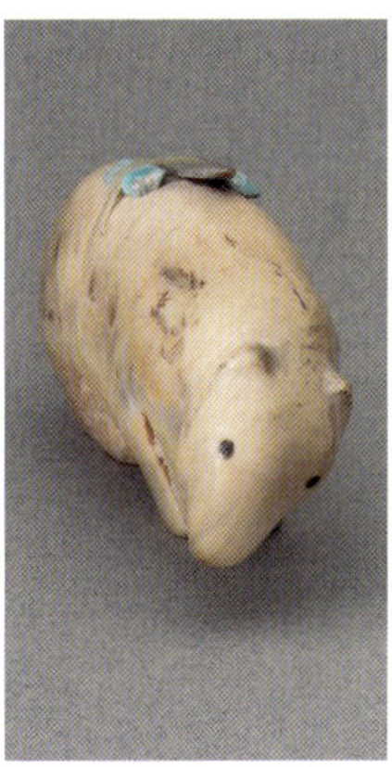

4. Ricolite serpentine bear. Length 2¾ inches. Collection of Andrews Pueblo Pottery.

5. Alabaster bear with painted and incised heart-line. Length 6 inches. Private collection.

6. Zuni rock bear. Length 3⅛ inches. Private collection.

7. Left: serpentine ram. Length 3½ inches. Private collection. Right: pipestone bear. Length 2¾ inches. Collection of Roger and Mary Crabtree.

8. Left: serpentine turtle. Length 2 inches. Right: serpentine turtle. Length 2⅛ inches. Private collections.

9. Turquoise turtle. Length 1⅛ inches. Collection of Roger and Mary Crabtree.

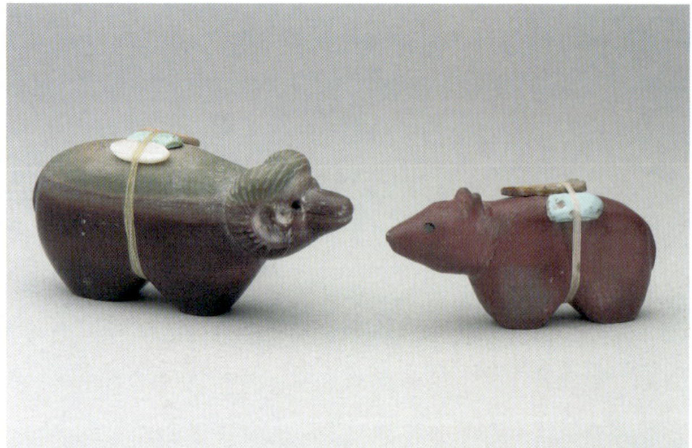

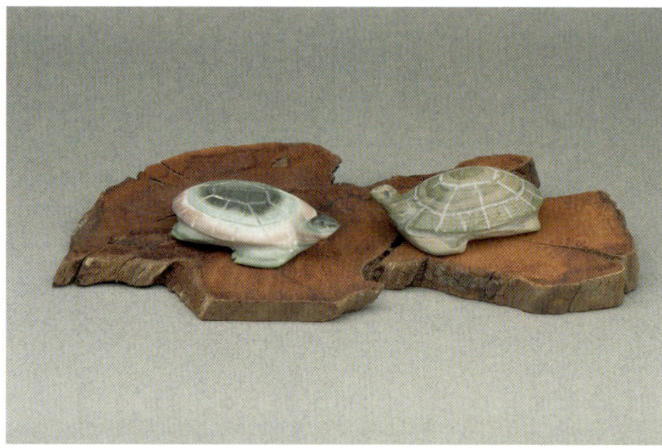

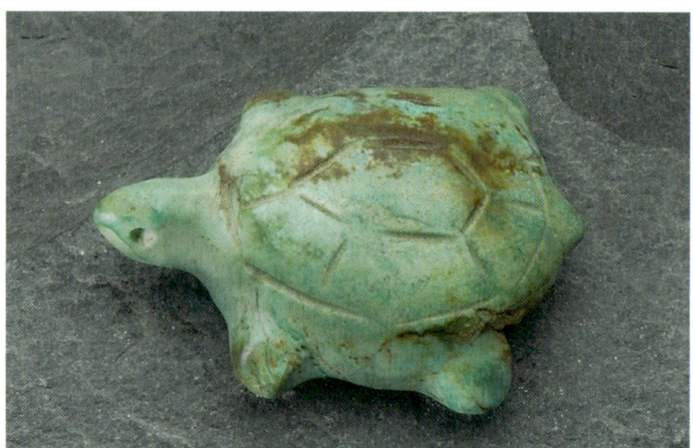

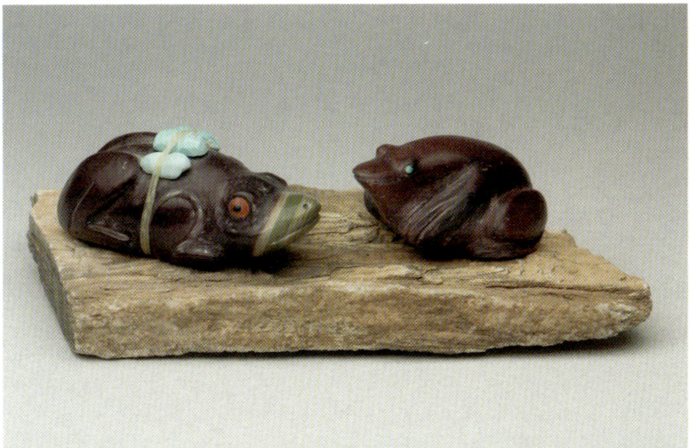

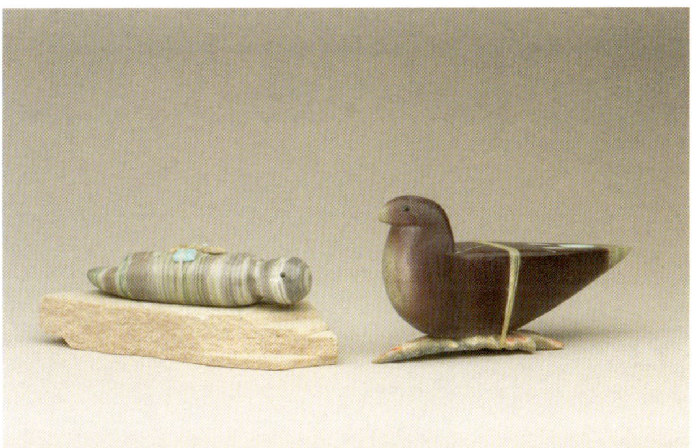

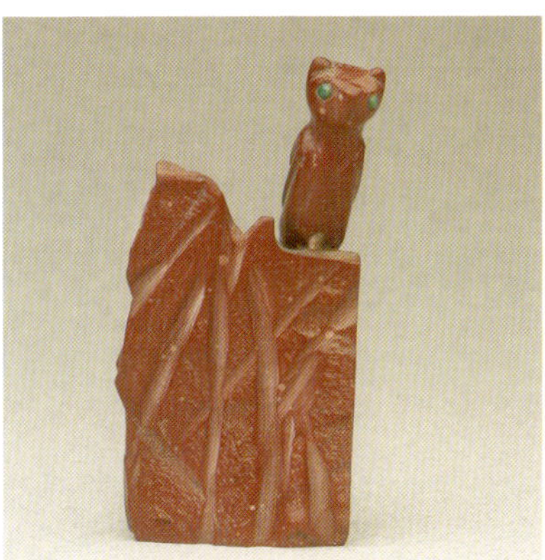

10. Left: serpentine frog. Length 3 inches. Collection of Grey Dog Trading Company. Right: Nutria travertine frog. Length 2½ inches. Private collection.

11. Left: serpentine eagle. Length 3 inches. Right: serpentine eagle. Length 3½ inches. Private collections.

12. Pipestone owl and perch. Height 2½ inches. Private collection.

13. Serpentine jay. Height 2¼ inches. Collection of Grey Dog Trading Company.

14. Green sea snail shell parrot and perch. Height 2½ inches. Private collection.

15. Pink conch shell bird. Length 6 inches. Private collection.

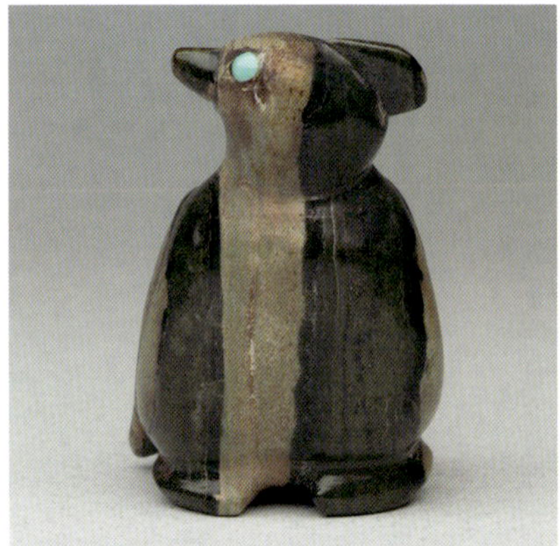

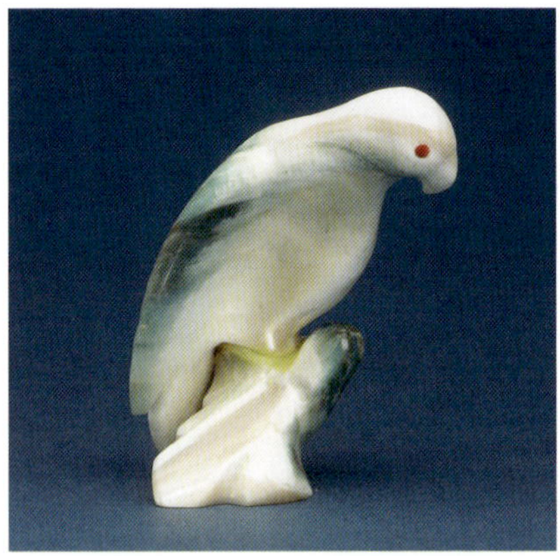

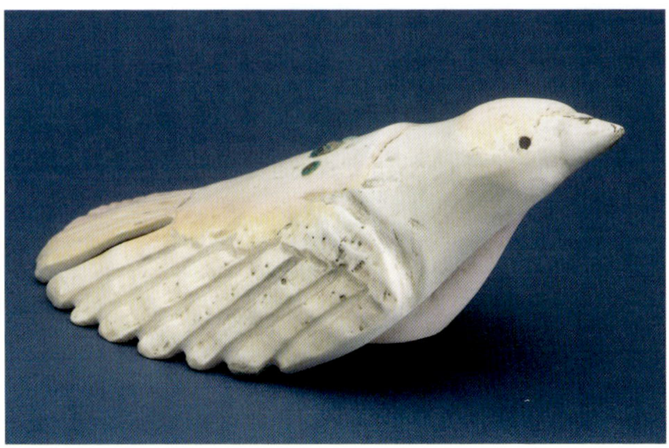

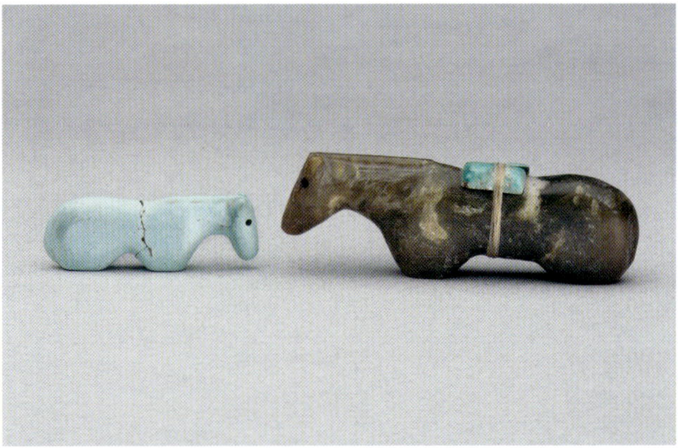

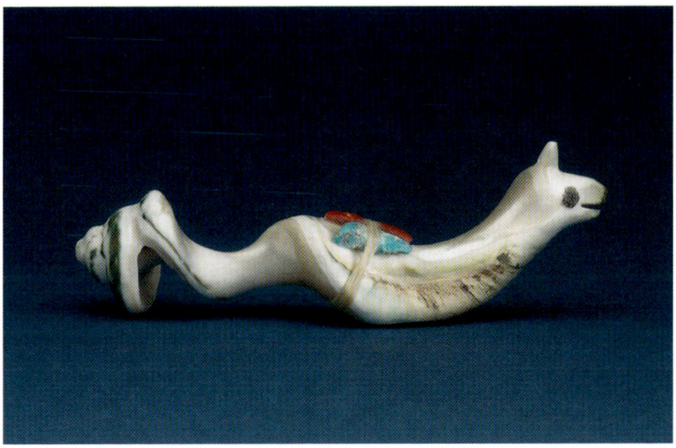

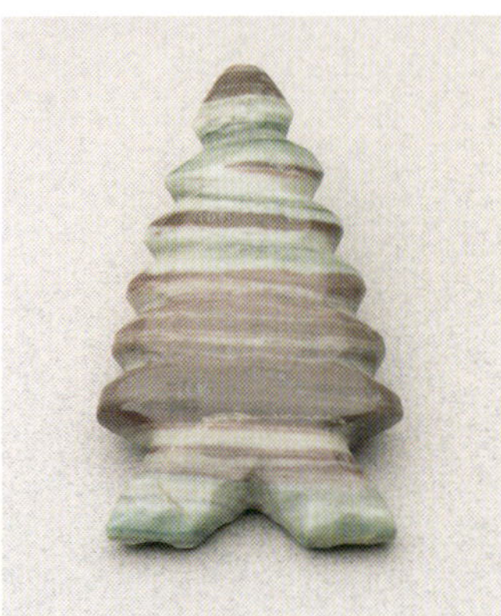

16. Left: natural turquoise horse. Length 1⅝ inches. Right: serpentine horse. Length 2⅝ inches. Private collection.

17. Green sea snail shell water serpent. Length 4 inches. Private collection.

18. Serpentine arrowhead. Length 2⅝ inches. Private collection.

Mary Tsikewa

1. Left: serpentine wolf. Length 1¾ inches. Private collection. Right: serpentine wolf. Length 4⅜ inches. Collection of Grey Dog Trading Company.

2. Left: serpentine wolf. Length 4¼ inches. Right: serpentine wolf. Length 2¾. Private collection.

3. Serpentine wolf or coyote. Length 2 inches. Private collection.

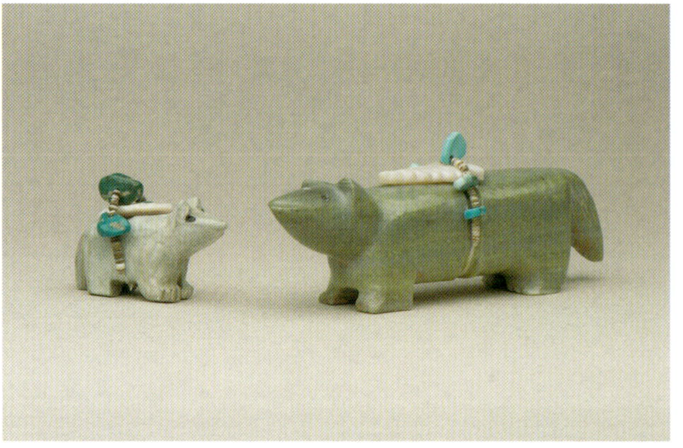

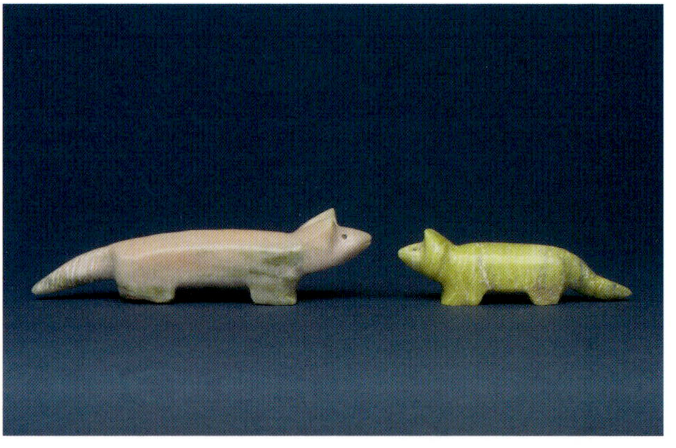

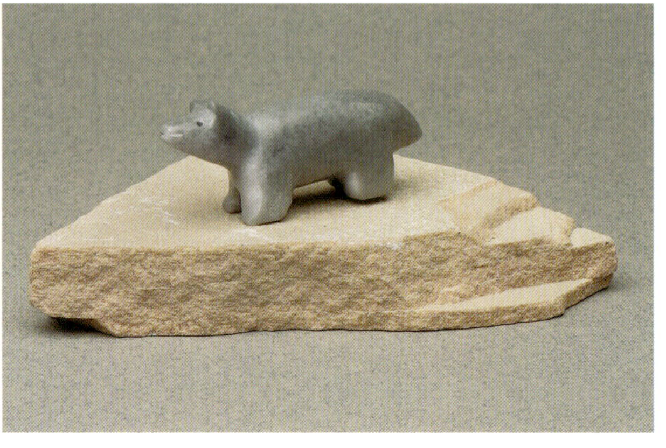

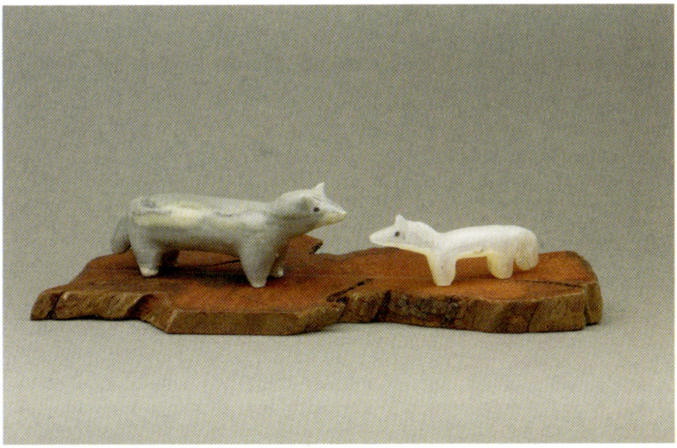

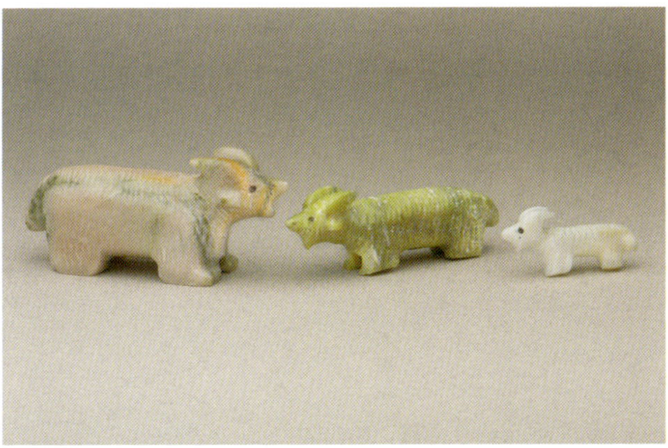

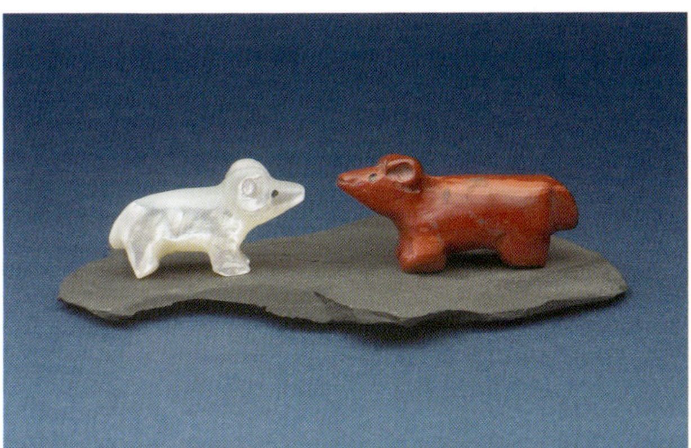

4. Left: serpentine horse. Length 3¼ inches. Collection of Grey Dog Trading Company. Right: mother-of-pearl horse. Length 2 inches. Private collection.

5. Left: serpentine goat. Length 3¼ inches. Collection of Roger and Mary Crabtree. Center: serpentine goat. Length 2⅞ inches. Private collection. Right: mother-of-pearl goat. Length 1⅝ inches. Collection of Roger and Mary Crabtree.

6. Left: mother-of-pearl ram. Length 1⅜. Private collection. Right: pipestone ram. Length 1⅝ inches. Collection of Roger and Mary Crabtree.

7. Turquoise frog. Length $1\frac{5}{8}$ inches. Collection of Dick Wessman.

8. Two-strand fetish necklace with birds of serpentine, travertine, marble, and dolomite, strung on olive shell heishi. Longest strand $28\frac{1}{2}$ inches. Collection of Challis L. Thiessen.

9. Detail of fetish necklace. Collection of Challis L. Thiessen.

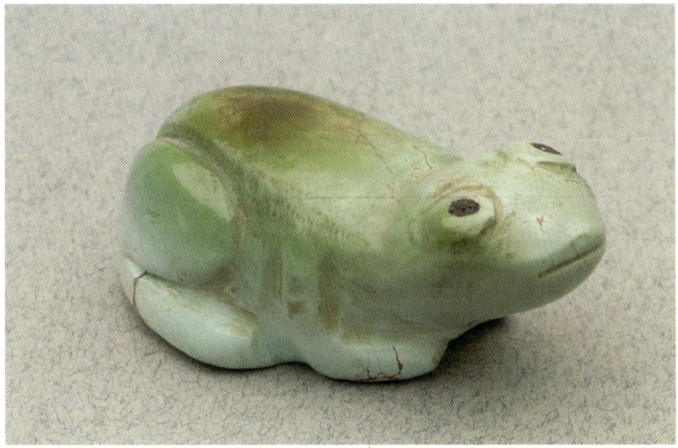

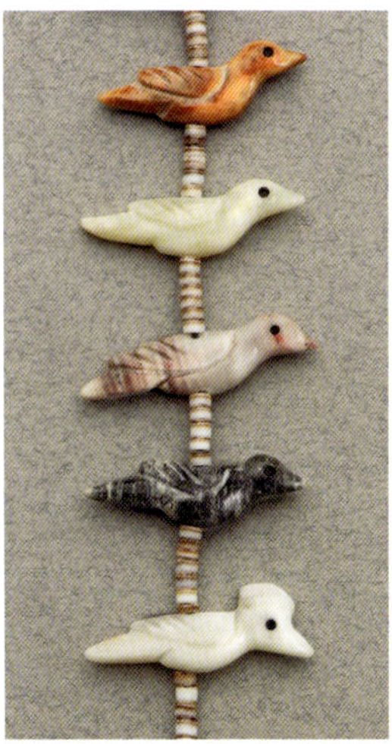

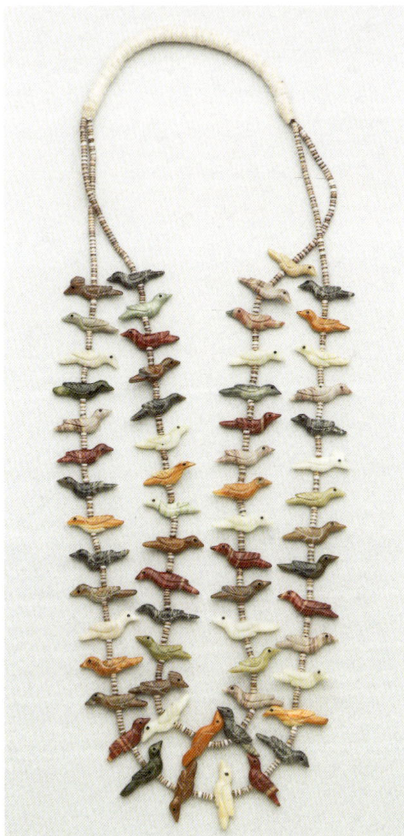

Bill Tsikewa

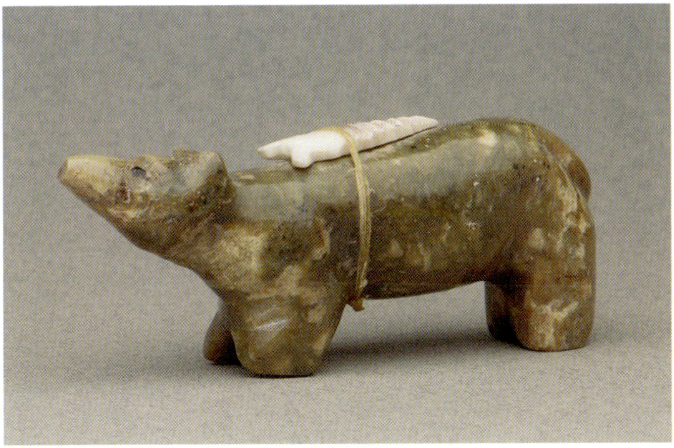

1. Serpentine bear. Length 3⅜ inches. Wheelwright Museum of the American Indian purchase in memory of Challis L. Thiessen.

David Tsikewa, Jr.

1. Three-strand fetish necklace with birds and wolves of mother-of-pearl, abalone, pink mussel shell, coral, turquoise, jet, pipestone, cowrie shell, and serpentine, strung on olive shell heishi. Longest strand 28¼ inches. Collection of Challis L. Thiessen.

2. Detail of fetish necklace. Collection of Challis L. Thiessen.

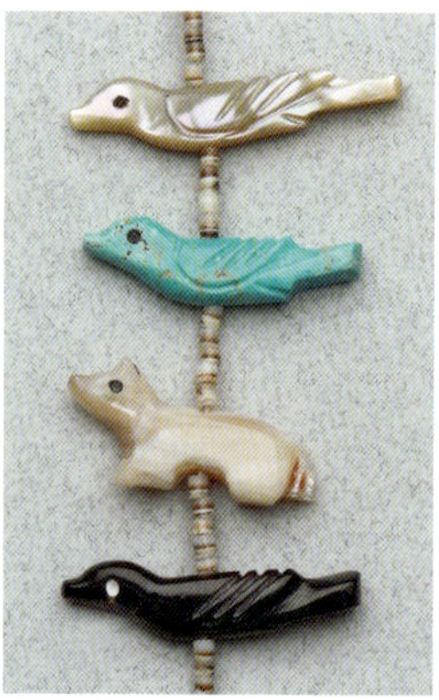

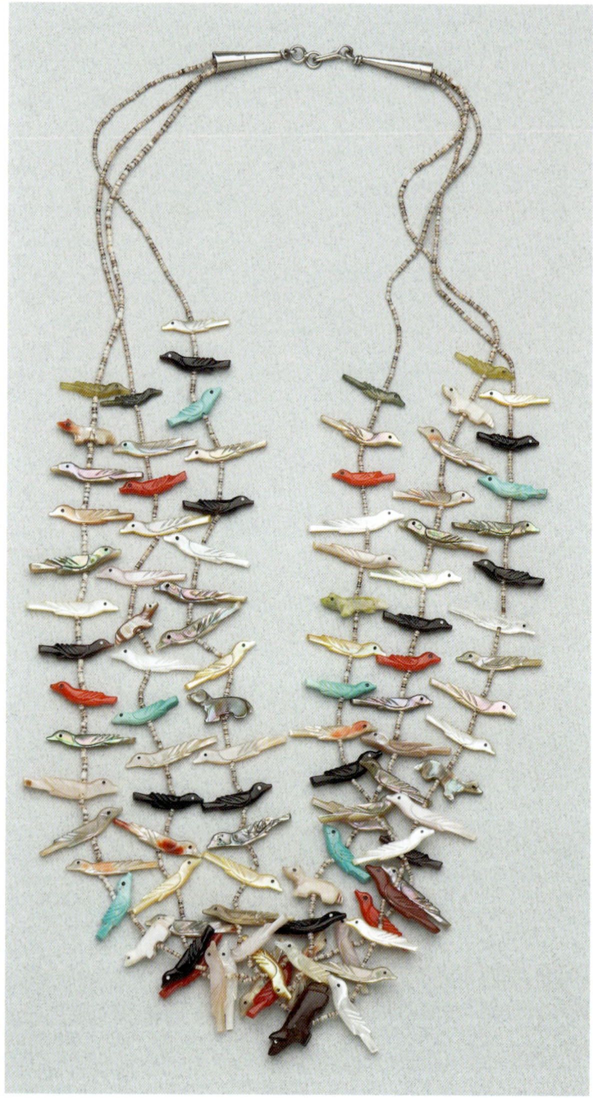

Lavina Kaskalla

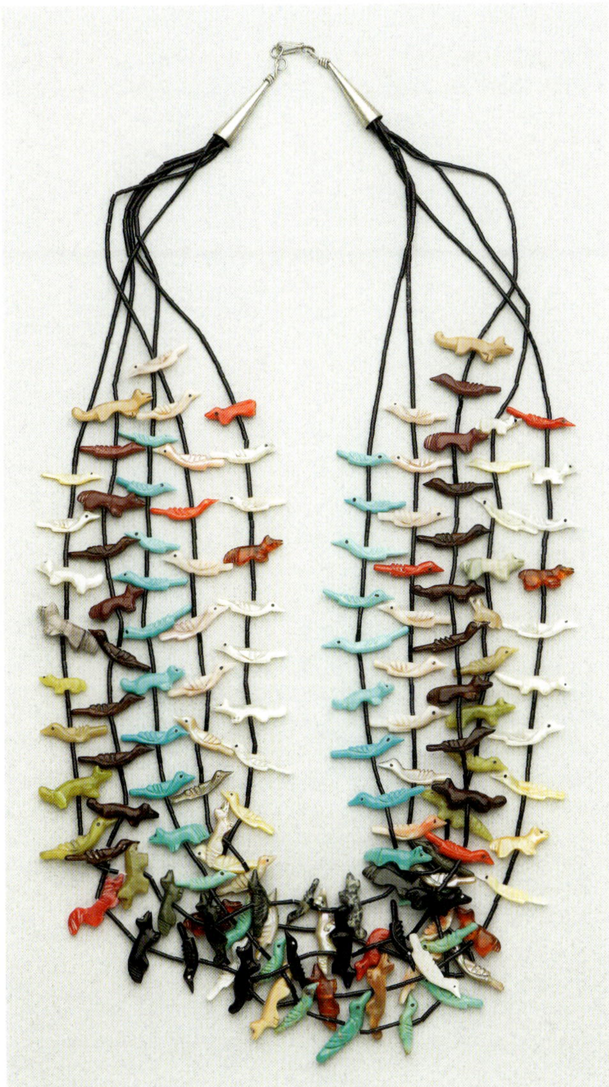

1. Five-strand fetish necklace with birds, foxes, wolves, and bears of pink mussel shell, turquoise, serpentine, mother-of-pearl, coral, jet, abalone, amber, cameo shell, and ironwood, strung on jet heishi. Longest strand 28½ inches. Collection of Challis L. Thiessen.

2. Detail of fetish necklace. Collection of Challis L. Thiessen.

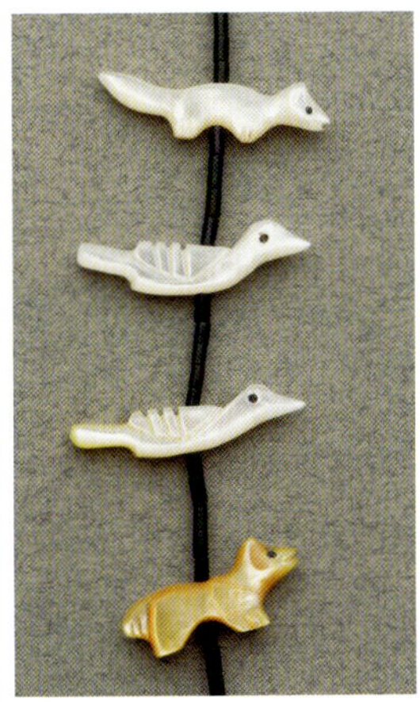

Leonard Kaskalla

1. Left: travertine horse. Length $3\frac{1}{8}$ inches. Private collection. Center: serpentine horse. Length $2\frac{1}{2}$ inches. Collection of Grey Dog Trading Company. Right: serpentine horse. Length $1\frac{3}{4}$ inches. Private collection.

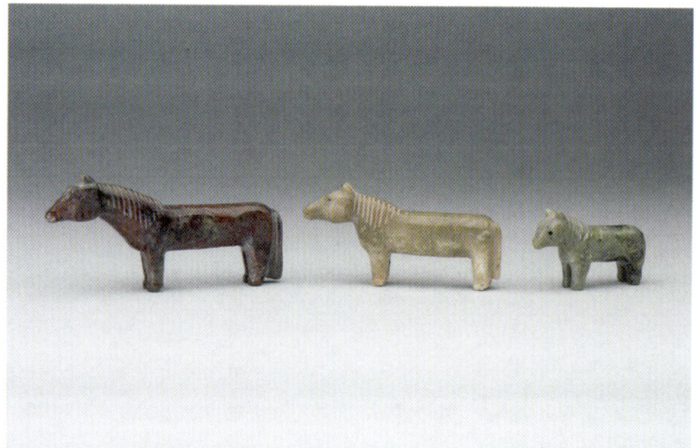

Rudy Tsikewa

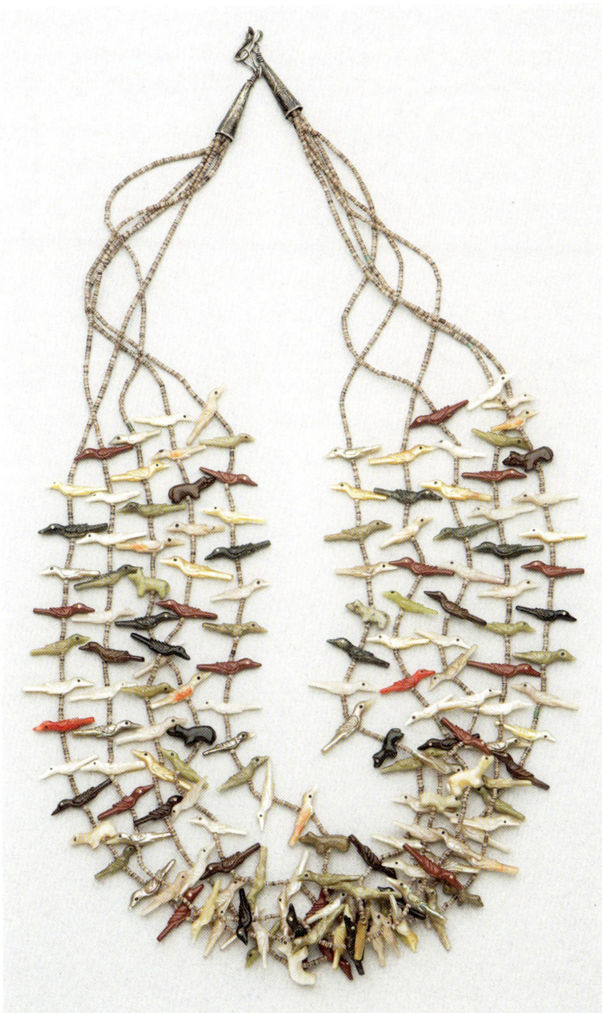

1. Five-strand fetish necklace with birds and bears of pipestone, jet, serpentine, abalone, mother-of-pearl, and coral, strung on olive shell heishi. Longest strand 29 inches. Collection of Challis L. Thiessen.

2. Detail of fetish necklace. Collection of Challis L. Thiessen.

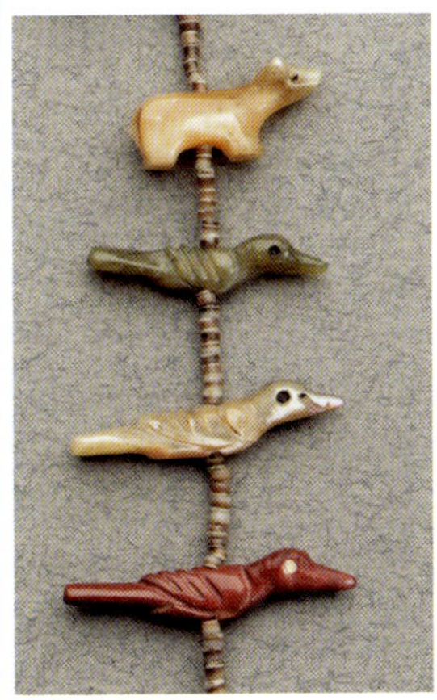

BIBLIOGRAPHY

Cushing, Frank Hamilton

1883 Zuni Fetiches. Pp. 3–45 in *Second Annual Report of the Bureau of Ethnology to the Secretary of the Smithsonian Institution, 1880–'81*. Washington.

Eggan, Fred and T. N. Pandey

1979 Zuni History, 1850–1970. Pp. 474–481 in *The Southwest*. Alfonso Ortiz, ed. *Handbook of North American Indians* 9. William C. Sturtevant, gen.ed. Washington: Smithsonian Institution.

McManis, Kent

2003 *Zuni Fetish Carvers: The Mid-Century Masters*. Santa Fe: Wheelwright Museum of the American Indian.

2004 *Zuni Fetishes and Carvings*. Tucson: Rio Nuevo Publishers.

Rodee, Marian and James Ostler

1990 *The Fetish Carvers of Zuni*. Albuquerque: The Maxwell Museum of Anthropology, University of New Mexico; and Zuni: The Pueblo of Zuni Arts and Crafts.

Thomas, Elaine Dodson

1997 *Prayer Warriors: Andrew and Effa Vander Wagen in Zuni*. Zuni: Elaine Dodson Thomas.

1997 *Shiwi Vander Wagens: Family Memories*. Zuni: Elaine Dodson Thomas.